Becoming An Executive Coachee: Creating Learning Partnerships

By Michael Carroll & Maria Gilbert

We would like to thank James Cannon, Pilar Gonzalez Doupe-Grey, John Nixon and Simon Cavicchia for reviewing and giving feedback on initial drafts of this manual.

Print Edition Published in 2008 by Vukani Publishing
www.vukanipublishing.co.uk

ISBN: 978-0-9551139-1-8

Printed in England

Contents

Section 1

Chapter 1

Chapter 2

Chapter 3

Chapter 4

Section 2

Chapter 5

Chapter 6

Chapter 7

Chapter 8

Chapter 9

Chapter 10

Chapter 11

Chapter 12

Section 3

Appendices

Declaration Of Executive Coachee Rights

As an executive coachee, you have the right to:

1. Be respected for being a professional.
2. Become the professional you can be (and not a clone of your coach).
3. A confidential setting where you feel safe to share what you need to.
4. A healthy coaching relationship with professional boundaries.
5. Fair and honest evaluations and reports.
6. See your coach's reports on you with opportunity to comment on the contents.
7. Know what your coach thinks of you and your work.
8. Make good any areas of development outlined by your coach.
9. Clear and focused feedback from your executive coach.
10. Give clear and focused feedback to your coach.
11. Ongoing, regular and systematic reviews of the coaching arrangement.
12. Learn in a way that suits your particular learning style.
13. Negotiate the coaching contract(s) (and knowing, in advance, what is nonnegotiable in the contract).
14. Mediation should the coaching relationship break down.
15. Appeal against decisions made in coaching with which you have problems.
16. Know and be part of any decisions made by your organization and your coach.

Declaration Of Executive Coachee Responsibilities

As an executive coachee, you have responsibility for/to:

1. Your own learning.
2. Preparing for coaching.
3. Using coaching time effectively (managing time boundaries).
4. Presenting yourself and your work openly and honestly.
5. Delivering the best service possible to your organization.
6. Creating learning partnerships with your coach and your organization.
7. Applying learning from your coaching to your performance at work.
8. Being aware of other stakeholders in the coaching arrangements eg., the team you work in, your organization, professional bodies.
9. Monitoring and evaluating your own work.
10. Reflecting on your work.
11. Feedback to yourself and to others (eg., your organization).
12. Being aware of cultural, religious, racial and sexual orientation differences between you and others.

Why This Manual?

There is a deluge of books on executive coaching and many of them, most of them indeed, are written for executive coaches. There is almost nothing for the executive coachee (the person receiving coaching). Coaching from the perspective of the coachee is, by and large, left to chance. This point has been made recently, "Looking at the literature and research on coaching, it is noticeable that while there is a considerable amount of emphasis placed on the skills of the coach, there seems to be less focus on the skills that a client needs for the coaching to be effective" (Stokes, 2007). This manual hopes to change that and offer coachees a systematic and organized approach to becoming an effective coachee – ie. becoming a partner in a learning journey and not simply the passive recipient of coaching services.

We do not particularly like the word "coachee" but other terms such as "client" or even worse "patient" detract from the role of being the partner in a formal executive coaching relationship. So we are left with "executive coachee" until a better term comes along.

We have chosen to write this manual specifically for executive coachees. We are very aware of other forms of coaching particularly life coaching. We know also of team coaching, peer coaching and of course, the manager as coach. While many aspects of this manual will pertain to coachees in those various relationships and settings, we thought it would overcomplicate our task (and the focus of executive coachees) to try to be all inclusive and see coachees as similar across all aspects of coaching. This is not the case and the tasks, roles, relationships and focus points of different types of coaching differ. Life coaching rarely has an organization that pays the coach and which has an agenda for the executive coachee. Managerial coaching clearly has responsibilities that go well beyond the responsibilities of external coaches. For these reasons, we narrow our attention to executive coachees.

The focus of executive coaching is learning. Later in this manual we will look at the various kinds of learning which are the field of executive coaching. Within the coaching arrangements and relationship, coachees learn in order to give better quality service to their organization (company, organization, firm, and institute). Effective executive coaches are facilitators or providers of learning. They aim to create the kind of collaborative relationship and the sort of learning environment that sustains learning for coachees. Coaching is for coachees, not for coaches. Too often we have had to put up with coach-based executive coaching where coaches take most of the initiatives, are motivated by their own current hobby horses, dazzle with their wisdom and insights and take the spotlight off coachees. This manual aims to empower coachees to take responsibility for their coaching and for their learning and to persuade coaches and organizations that pay for coaching to allow them to do so.

This manual is primarily for executive coachees. We consider a coachee to be anyone, of any profession, who is the recipient of a coaching arrangement where the focus of the coaching work is the professional development of the executive.

It is still rare for coachees to receive help and instruction in being effective coachees. There is little literature to which coachees can turn that is written specifically for them to help them make sense of, understand and be a collaborative partner in the coaching arrangement, either one to one or in a group/team.

Hence this manual. For coachees (and for coaches and supervisors of coaches who want to know about being coachees), it will lead you through the various stages of understanding, setting up, contracting for, maintaining and ending a coaching relationship. In "Training Supervisees how to Use Supervision", Inskipp (1999) suggests three reasons for concentrating on supervisees – we apply these same reasons to coachees:

1. To empower executive coachees.
2. To help coachees to be open and honest in what they bring to their executive coaching sessions (coaches can only work with what is brought to them).
3. To involve coachees actively in all aspects of executive coaching so creating a collaborative learning relationship. To do this coachees need skills, knowledge and practical ways of fulfilling their roles and responsibilities (Inskipp, 1999).

...while primarily for beginner coachees, this manual will also assist those who have been coached before...

Our hope is that executive coaches will give coachees this manual for the above reasons and also because there is not enough time spent on helping coachees use coaching effectively either on training courses or within coaching itself. However, while primarily for beginner coachees, this manual will also assist those who have been coached before. Indeed experienced coachees might find it helpful to review how they take part in the coaching relationship and help them look again at the various processes involved. It is too easy for all of us, no matter how experienced, to follow meaningless routines in our work no matter what our profession. Executive coaching interrupts our work (and sometimes our mindlessness) in order to help us reflect on it and thereby, do it differently and better. Executive coaching is as much about creativity as it is about skills and competencies. This manual will provide a springboard for discussion (it cannot be an end in itself) between/amongst coachees and coaches so that they end up with the same understanding of coaching and can be invested in the same coaching outcomes.

Reading The Manual: Making It Work For You

This manual is not intended to be read straight through from beginning to end. Different sections of it will be of help at different times in a coachee's life. We have divided the manual into three sections to make it more accessible. Section 1 is for beginning executive coachees who may well be thinking about executive coaching for the first time and entering their first coaching arrangements. It contains the basics of understanding coaching and being involved in choosing an executive coach (though some coachees do not have that choice) as well as contracting and preparing for coaching. Section 2 contains material more applicable and of use to those who have begun their executive coaching and have in place those elements discussed in Section 1. From the strength of a healthy coaching relationship, they can now look to other elements within coaching to enhance their learning of secondary skills (learning about developmental stages in coaching, learning about "drivers" and about developing emotional literacy skills amongst others). Section 3 is an Appendix which includes a number of exercises and frameworks to help executive coachees as they move forward in their coaching journey. Choose whichever suits you and makes sense at your stage of being a coachee.

While this book is intended as a guide to facilitate executive coaches to be part of the coaching process, there are a number of areas that it will not consider. Not because these areas are not important – some of them are crucial to the effectiveness of executive coaching – but because they may or may not be of direct concern to you, the coachee. However, we have no way of knowing which aspects of the big picture of executive coaching are your direct concern and which are not, so here are a few pointers to further information and reading if they concern you:

1. Why coaching is so popular today and the influences on coaching as a viable and effective intervention (see Jarvis, Lane and Fillery-Travis, 2006: Chapter 1).
2. Does Coaching work? Looking at the research evidence (see Jarvis, Lane and Fillery-Travis, 2006: chapter 4; Passmore and Gibbes, 2007: The state of Executive Coaching Research: What does the current literature tell us?) There are two further summaries for those interested in up to date research on the effectiveness of executive coaching: Chapter 4 in the Handbook of Coaching Psychology (2007) and "Advances in research in Coaching Outcomes" (Grief, 2007).
3. Coaching surveys looking at the percentage of organizations using coaching, why organizations use coaching, what is involved in the delivery of coaching, does coaching work, the benefits of coaching (CIPD, Training and Development Survey Reports, 2004, 2005, 2006).
4. Making Coaching Work: Creating a Coaching Culture (Clutterbuck and Megginson, 2005).
5. Coaching and Buying Coaching Services (Jarvis, CIPD, 2004)
6. Team Coaching (Clutterbuck, 2007).

While this manual hopes to "empower" executive coachees in all aspects of their coaching arrangements, we are all too aware that some executive coaches and some organizations will not be coachee focused. Quite the opposite, in our experience. There are coaches who see little point in "negotiating" with coachees and will consider it their task to tell coachees what executive coaching is and how they (coachees) should involve themselves in it. They fit coachees to their models and theories rather than consider which models and theories best apply to this individual. Some hierarchical-based organizations will have little interest in setting up "learning partnerships" but will work on the expert-beginner model of executive coaching ie., that it is the task of executive coaches to tell coachees how to do their work and guide and monitor that work often concentrating on articulating weaknesses as a way of progressing personal and professional development. We do not want to put coachees in a "no-win" situation, pretending that they will be partners in a learning endeavour when there is little chance of that happening. Having said that, we want to outline an understanding of executive coaching that, in our view, is based on solid principles of adult learning and will add value to both coachees and their organizations while making executive coaching a much more interesting engagement for coaches.

...Executive Coaching exists to support the personal and professional learning of executive coachees...

Executive Coaching exists to support the personal and professional learning of executive coachees and, thereby contribute to the goals of their organizations (we repeat from above). Part of that learning is about accountability. Coaching is a process that offers accountability or responsibility to whoever (professions, authorities, managers, organizations, tax payers, managers, investors etc) that coachees take their work seriously enough to set up a reflective space where they review that work, learn from it and apply that learning when they return to it. Eventually, they will become reflective practitioners who reflect-in-action (think about the work as they do the work) and move towards being full time self learners.

Connor and Pokora (2007) are two of the few authors who devote time to helping coachees use coaching to best effect. Chapter 3 in their book is entitled "How can I be an effective client?" and the summary of their chapter is worth remembering as a fine guide about what to keep in mind in order to get the best from your executive coaching.

1. "Getting the right coach or mentor".
2. "Knowing yourself".
3. "Having realistic expectations".
4. "Negotiating a working agreement".
5. "Thinking ahead and being strategic".

6. "Being proactive".
7. "Learning from support and challenge".
8. "Using reflective space".
9. "Developing your imagination".
10. "Identifying your resources and working smart".
11. "Setting goals and making action plans".
12. "Developing skills, making changes and delivering results".

(Connor and Pokora, 2007:54).

Chapter 1

Overview Of Executive Coaching

What Is An Executive Coachee?

A coachee, at its simplest, is a person (or a team) who is the recipient of coaching services. As a coachee, you have two initial issues to face that make all the difference in the outcome of coaching for you:

1. Understanding what executive coaching is.
2. Choosing to be a coachee in a coaching arrangement.

...Being clear about what is executive coaching and what is involved in being a coachee in such an endeavour is vital if coaching is going to work for you...

Being clear about what is executive coaching and what is involved in being a coachee in such an endeavour is vital if coaching is going to work for you. Not only are your expectations and your learning at stake but it is equally important that others involved in your coaching arrangement (your company and your coach) have a similar understanding of executive coaching. All three parties (or four if there is a coaching organization involved) need to be "singing from the same hymn sheet" – otherwise, in our experience, all sorts of problems emerge around differing expectations.

Example

Gillian's HR Director suggested she take part in a coaching arrangement he was setting up for senior executives. He told her that coaching was to help her in her new role as Head of Marketing with a new and extended team of 25 people. Gillian thought this a great idea and looked forward to meeting her new coach. The HR director had mentioned to the Executive Coach (who was a member of ExCoach Supreme, a well known Executive Coaching provider) that he wanted him to concentrate on Gillian's delegation skills. At the first meeting Gillian suggested that she would like to work on Marketing Strategy as the main focus of executive coaching. Her new coach, after the first meeting, feels that he and she should concentrate on building the new team.

The above example shows how differing agendas (in this case three different agendas at work) are a recipe for potential danger and we can imagine the outcomes as the HR director, Gillian and the Executive Coach all work from different expectations. Soon we will look at how you can come to an understanding of what executive coaching means for you but for now it's worth remembering there are other "players" in the executive coaching game whose agendas need to be accommodated.

A further key issue for you is CHOOSING executive coaching. You are a coachee. That means, in our view, that you have chosen to work with another person called an executive coach (or with others, as in a group or team coaching) to develop yourself professionally and to release your potential. There are a number of assumptions in the statement we have just made:

1. That you have "chosen" executive coaching.
2. That you know how to use executive coaching to impact your performance.
3. That you feel safe and supported being an executive coachee in this coaching relationship.
4. That you want to learn from being an executive coachee.
5. That you can trust your coach.

Exercise

*You might want to put down this booklet and think about
some questions around those assumptions:*

1. *Is executive coaching something you "have to do" rather
   than a process "you have chosen to engage with"?*
2. *What has been your experience of coaching to date (as a
   coachee), if you have already been in coaching?*
3. *What immediately comes to your mind when you
   think of the term "executive coaching"?*
4. *Do you have a clear understanding of what executive coaching means?*
5. *Have you considered how you learn and what learning style is best suited to you?*
6. *Has anyone ever talked to you about, or have you thought
   about, how to use coaching most effectively?*
7. *Is your view of coaching affected by other one-to-one situations
   you have experienced (eg., counselling, supervision)*
8. *What "risks" may you be letting yourself in for in accepting
   (choosing) to be an executive coachee?*

Let's look at some of your answers to these questions.

*If your answer to the first question was that executive coaching is something you "have to
do", is mandatory because of the requirements of your work, and that is the only reason
you involve yourself in it, PLEASE think again. Our experience is that doing something
because you are required to do so rarely reaps as many benefits as it can. Sometimes quite
the opposite – it blocks real learning and you will go through the procedure without heart
or choice. You might even end up sabotaging the whole arrangement and making sure it
does not work. Without apology we ask you to consider choosing to be a full participant
in executive coaching, even if it is requirement. Don't accept executive coaching "in
bad faith", ie., as an imposition or a requirement or a mandatory exercise – to do so will
seriously and negatively affect your motivation, your commitment and your cooperation.*

*...If you have
been allocated an
executive coach
you might like to
look at helpful
hints on how
to handle this
relationship...*

Choose executive coaching – it will make all the difference regarding
your motivation and cooperation and thus lead to more openness and
learning. If you have been allocated an executive coach you might like to
look at helpful hints on how to handle this relationship on page 31.

If your experience of executive coaching has been that it has been led totally or
almost totally by the executive coach rather than coachee-oriented, then we are
hoping that you might take a more **proactive** stance in regard to negotiating
what you want and need from executive coaching. Our hope is that the coach
you have chosen or has been appointed to you will move towards you, not
insist that you move to join them in their way of learning and teaching.

We are also keen to help you **review your understanding** of executive
coaching and what it has meant to you in the past.

And we will keep coming back to the focus of **learning** as the central aspect of
executive coaching (not monitoring, or assessing, or evaluating, or giving feedback
– all important dimensions of executive coaching but not its key purpose).

Some of you reading this manual will be beginning executives who are in the process of learning how best to be a leader or manager and who need the forum provided by an experienced person (executive coach) to allow you to think through, reflect on and mull over the issues, problems and joys, that emerge from the work you are doing. Others of you will be more experienced leaders or managers. Whether beginning or experienced, in the conversation called "executive coaching" you will look inwards to what is happening to you as you work and look outwards to how the work is being done. From these reflections will come learning which will be used to increase the effectiveness of your work.

...Even though roles and responsibilities can be different, the essence of all executive coaching is the same...

What makes an executive coachee an effective coachee is a desire and wish to learn from opening up their work to an executive coach so that in the ensuing conversation new thoughts, insights, awareness, ideas, feelings, approaches and theories will create better performance. Hence, we see the worlds of mentoring, consultation and executive counselling as closely allied to the world of executive coaching. We also see links here with line-management. Even though roles and responsibilities can be different, the essence of all executive coaching is the same: For the executive coach the question is: How can I, as an executive coach, facilitate the learning, knowledge and performance of coachees? From a coachee's perspective the question is similar: How can I, as an executive coachee, present and reflect on my work in the safe and facilitating environment of a healthy coaching relationship so that I can learn to be more professionally effective?

What Is Executive Coaching?

While understanding the meaning of executive coaching is essential for coachees, the literature does not always help here. There is some confusion about what executive coaching actually is and an abundance of definitions and descriptions exist. All the more reason for spending time on developing your own "philosophy of executive coaching" ie. What is at the heart of executive coaching?

Here are a few definitions to get the mind working:

"Executive coaching is an action-learning process to enhance effective action and learning agility. It involves a professional relationship and a deliberate personalized process to provide an executive with valid information, free and informed choices based on that information, and internal commitment to those choices" (Witherspoon 2000: 167).

Kilburg (1996: 143) puts it differently: "Coaching is a helping relationship formed between a client with managerial authority and responsibility in an organization and a consultant who uses a wide variety of behavioural techniques and methods to help the client achieve a mutually identified set of goals to improve personal performance and personal satisfaction, and consequently to improve the effectiveness of the client's organization within a formal defined coaching agreement".

Jarvis (CIPD, 2004) reminds us that coaching refers to many different activities and puts her understanding of coaching much more simply as: "A means of developing people within an organization in order that they perform more effectively and reach their potential "(p. 17). She has a list of further definitions and then gathers a number of the features of executive coaching together (p. 18):

1. "It consists of one to one developmental discussions".
2. "It provides people with feedback on both their strengths and weaknesses".
3. "It aims at specific issues/areas".

4. "It is a relatively short-term activity".
5. "It is essentially a nondirective form of development".
6. "It focuses on improving performance and developing/enhancing individual skills".
7. "It is used to address a wide range of issues".
8. "Coaching activities have both organizational and individual goals".
9. "It assumes that the individual is psychologically healthy and does not require a clinical intervention".
10. "It works on the premise that clients are self aware, or can achieve self-awareness".
11. "It is time-boundaried".
12. "It is a skilled activity".
13. "Personal issues may be discussed but the emphasis is on performance at work" (pp.18-19).

Sperry (2004) draws a distinction between four types of interventions one of which is executive coaching:

1. Executive psychotherapy – focus is on the person and his/her growth and is delivered by a trained counsellor, psychologist or psychotherapist.
2. Executive training and development: focus is on skills, knowledge and delivered by a teacher or trainer.
3. Executive consultation: focus is on the external organizational issues and delivered by an experienced organizational adviser.
4. Executive Coaching: focus is on work performance and delivered by a person trained in developing work potential (knowledge, skills, competencies, qualities of the executive).

For those of you interested in looking in more detail at the differences between counselling and coaching then the best summary, in our view, is the article, "A Bridge over Troubled Water: Bringing together coaching and Counselling" in Counselling at Work (Bachkirova and Cox, 2005). There are also summaries in Bluckett (2006) and Hawkins and Smith (2006).

"Executive Coaching is the process of equipping people with the tools, knowledge and opportunities they need to develop themselves and become more effective" (Peterson, 1996 – quoted in Sperry p. 10).

Executive Coaching: "A coach works collaboratively with an executive to accomplish specific goals and objectives involving the executive's productivity and well-being: typically focuses on increasing skills and performance or on personal and professional development; usually of short duration" (p. 5).

(There are a few more definitions of executive coaching in Appendix 1).

...If you are feeling a bit confused at the moment, don't worry...

If you are feeling a bit confused at the moment, don't worry – join the large group of people who feel there is not an agreed or final definition of what makes up executive coaching. As you can see from the above, some concentrate on the person behind the professional first of all, while others focus on the professional and see what personal issues emerge. From all the definitions above a number of factors emerge that require consideration:

1. Executive coaching usually involves at least three systems: the organization or company, the Executive who is an employee of the company and the Executive Coach. Executive coaching in a triadic relationship and we forget the role of the Company or Organization in coaching to our peril.
2. The focus of coaching is the performance of the Executive.

3. The three systems work together to contract so that they are all clear and agreed about what areas of performance need centring on during executive coaching.
4. Coaching is a formal, contracted relationship where the roles and responsibilities of all parties are clear: it is a form of relational learning.
5. Executive coach and coachee meet (contact may be by phone or email as well as being face-to-face) and converse about how the executive can develop his/her potential. These thoughtful or vital conversations are the heart blood of executive coaching
6. The coaching dyad (executive coach and coachee) and the organization evaluate progress (according to criteria agreed beforehand).

Focus Points Of Executive Coaching

We mentioned earlier in this chapter that executive coaching equals learning. While we will return to learning in a later chapter we would like to present some focus points of learning here. A few of them are:

1. Knowledge.
2. Skills and Competencies.
3. Learning from Experience.
4. Learning how to Learn.
5. Transformational Learning.

A quick look at each of these will help:

1. Knowledge

...it is the task of executive coaching to evaluate what domains of knowledge are needed by the coachee...

While Executive coaches are not necessarily experts and may not even know more than their coachees (in many, perhaps most areas, coachees will be more expert than their executive coaches), it is the task of executive coaching to evaluate what domains of knowledge are needed by the coachee and whether or not he/she has the necessary knowledge to do his/her job effectively, or more effectively. While it may not be the task of the Executive Coach to give this knowledge, it is their task to look at how it can be found and integrated into the working life of the executive. By knowledge, we mean information, theories, frameworks and models that help executives do their jobs.

2. Skills And Competencies

Again, direct coaching in skills and competencies can be integral to executive coaching. Helping an Executive learn the skills of leading a meeting or writing a report or dealing with a difficult member of staff are all "teachable". A skill is the ability to do something.

Hawkins and Smith (2006: 123 and 206) draw a distinction between skills, competencies, capability and capacity:

"Competencies we see as the ability to use a skill or use a tool.

Capability refers to the ability to use the tool or skill, at the right time, in the right way in the right place;

Capacity is a human quality such as flexibility, warmth, engagement, imagination etc rather than a skill and has more to do with how you are rather than what you do" (p.123).

Their model connecting these with learning is helpful (Table 7.1, page 124)

Skills	Performance	Development	Transformation
Competence	Capability	Capacity in Level	Capacity shift between levels

Figure 1.1: Skills and Competencies Model (Hawkins and Smith, 2006)

Coaching for qualities brings executive coaching into a different domain – it now requires looking at areas such as interpersonal skills, confidence, self-management, managerial abilities, assertiveness, and a range of other competencies that could be called "emotional competencies" (see Goleman and our later section on Learning Emotional Awareness).

3. Learning From Experience

...Executive coaching, in our view, spends most of its time here, learning from experience...

Executive coaching, in our view, spends most of its time here, learning from experience. How can we help executives use their own experience to teach them how to be better at their jobs? This is about "learning from doing" or "becoming students of our own experience... sitting at the feet of our work" (Zachary, 2002: xv). We will return to this later in this chapter in a fuller way.

4. Learning How To Learn

(Go to Chapter 6 for a full review of learning how to learn).

5. Transformational Learning

We see transformational learning as a process in which you employ your capabilities and expand your capacities for creativity and engagement in relation to work and relating to people in a way that completely transforms your performance. When describing the change process people talk of "doing more of the same" with regard to acquiring more similar skills and improving areas of performance; transformational change involves a radical restructuring of the way you think about and do things so that the new process is in no way similar to the former but introduces a new way of looking at things, of managing and of organising your workload. In terms of the 'old way of doing things' transformation may look completely 'crazy and illogical' because it challenges all of the fixed and historically-embedded assumptions of the organization. However, the change is aimed at radical restructuring and novel ways of thinking 'outside of the frame'.

For more on skills, performance, behaviour, development, transition and transformation see chapter 2 in Hawkins and Smith (2006).

Elements In Executive Coaching

These elements go to make up executive coaching.

1. A Forum For Reflection

Executive coaching is the forum where executives reflect on their work and learn from that reflection through their interaction with another who takes on the role of coach. It is play-back time. We look at the past to learn for the future. We mull over what has happened in order to learn from it and apply our learning when we go back to work. Later we will look in some detail at what reflection is and how executive coaches can become facilitators of reflection.

2. A Focus On Experiential Learning

Experiential learning is the type of learning most appropriate to executive coaching: not the only type, but the one most often used. Executive coaching is built on the reflection/action model where the actual work of the executive becomes the vehicle for learning. The Experiential Learning Cycle (Kolb, 1984) comprises four stages as shown in this diagram:

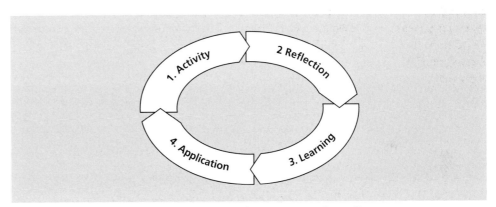

Figure 1.2: The Experiential Learning Cycle (Kolb, 1984)

The types or modes of learning featured at each stage of the experiential learning cycle are:

...We want to move as coachees to being unconsciously competent...

Doing or Activity (based on tacit knowledge). Here we know intuitively by accessing that store of sometimes unconscious knowledge we already have. We want to move as coachees to being unconsciously competent (from unconscious incompetence to conscious incompetence to conscious competence to unconscious competence) so that we access our tacit knowledge and involve ourselves in our work intuitively.

Reflection: Moving to experiential learning involves using reflection. Reflection and critical reflection learning engages coachees in honest consideration and investigation of their work. Coaches facilitate this reflection in order to help coachees learn from their own practice. With open mind and open heart (Scharmer, 2007), coachees are transparent, honest, aware and alert to what is happening as they reflect on the procedures, processes and relationships involved.

Propositional or Declarative Learning now emerges from critical reflection. Learning is articulated and connected to theory, frameworks, models and other intellectual definitions and descriptions.

Practical Knowledge emerges in the final section of the Experiential learning Cycle by finding ways of translating propositional learning into skills, capabilities, competencies and qualities of the coachee that enables him or her to return more skillfully to their work.

Executive Coachee and the Learning Cycle: Some questions for you to consider:

1. Executive Coachees **do** their work. How are you doing your work?
2. Executive Coachees **stop** doing their work and start **reflecting** on it. Are you able to reflect openly and honestly on your work?
3. Executive Coachees draw out their **learning** from their reflection. What are you learning?
4. Executive Coachees then **apply** their learning? Do you implement your learning? Do you integrate this learning into your work activities? What can you experiment with doing differently?

For a fuller version of the experiential learning cycle as applied to coaching we suggest you read Law, Ireland and Hussain (2007, 36-49).

Executives can get stuck at any stage of this process ie., they find themselves not able to engage in the activity, not able to reflect, not able to learn, not able to apply learning. The following are some examples of individuals stuck at the various points of the Experiential learning cycle.

...Executives can get stuck at any stage of this process...

Examples

Jane is so stressed and overworked that she is unable to do her work as she would like to. She is stuck at the Activity Stage.

Jack is so worried about getting it right and being seen to get it right that he cannot allow himself to consider areas of his work where he is not doing well. He is stuck at the Reflection Stage.

Jill gets stuck in the Learning Stage by not allowing herself to be vulnerable (and in a place of not knowing); she cannot ask for what she needs in her learning.

Jim comes up with great ideas but they never seem to get applied because he moves too fast and tries to do too much too quickly. He is stuck at the Implementation Stage.

Exercise

Go around the four stages of the Experiential Learning Cycle and see, at each stage, where and how you sometimes get stuck. What are you experiencing when you get stuck? Is this a familiar place for you?

Effective executive coaches facilitate the learning of coachees by ensuring that these blocks are dealt with and that learning continues around the Experiential Learning Cycle. A number of executive coaching features now emerge:

1. The focus of executive coaching is on the learning of coachees, ie., your learning. Hitherto the apprentice joined the master-practitioner, watched, learned, tried out the work, and was given feedback on how it should be done. They practiced and learned more. Power - the right way to do the job and how this was taught -resided in the hands of the master who was more experienced. The new emphasis is on the learning of coachees with executive coaches interested in questions such as: At what stage in their professional development are coachees? How do they best learn? What learning objectives supply the focus of coaching time? How are coachees integrating the various components of their training and experience?

2. Your main learning takes place through reflection on the actual work itself.

3. Your executive coach is primarily a "manager, provider or facilitator of learning" and hopefully asks questions such as: How can I, as coach, assist your learning?

4. Empowering you to be an active collaborator in the learning endeavour of coaching is essential for learning.

5. Executive coaching is an emotional experience as well as a rational one and the emotional aspect needs to be considered and worked with in coaching.

6. You will acquire your own style of being an executive or manager. There is no objective way of helping (as there is in becoming a carpenter, plumber or goldsmith, professions from which the apprenticeship models emerged). While there is a programme to be followed, participants learn their way of doing it. Executive coaching is needed so that individuals can forge their own identity within the overall boundaries of their organizations. Executive coaching is not about learning to do it as the coach does it, but about learning an individual and unique way of interacting with work.

7. You will go through stages on your journey to becoming an experienced and hopefully, wise executive. Your executive coach will perform various tasks as they work with you. If these tasks can be geared to the developmental stage through which you are travelling, then learning can be better managed and can be seen as cumulative.

...Executive coaching is needed so that individuals can forge their own identity within the overall boundaries of their organizations...

3. A Forum For Accountability

Executive coaching is a process where accountability to various stakeholders is considered (organizations, professional associations and those who pay for the work) and are assured that effectiveness and high quality is being maintained.

Your Own Philosophy Of Executive Coaching

At this stage, we hope you are ready to write your own "philosophy of executive coaching", ie., what it means to you. Can you capture in a paragraph what it might look like? One group of coachees used images and metaphors to capture what executive coaching meant to them and came up with the following:

For me executive coaching is:

1. "A torch – which illuminates my work".
2. "A container – where I feel safe and held".
3. "A mirror – where I see myself and my work (the mirror is usually held by my executive coach)".

4. "A playpen – where we play with ideas, feelings, intuitions, hunches, theories".
5. "A dance – where we learn how to work together in harmony".
6. "A classroom – which contains two learners one of whom facilitates my learning".
7. "A courtroom – where assessments, evaluations and judgments take place".
8. "A journey – where we both move through stages and need to decide where we are going, what we want to take with us, and what to leave behind".
9. "A thermometer – to gauge temperatures (intellectual, emotional, psychological and social climates)".
10. "A sculpture – where I am being fashioned into something yet to be".

Exercise

You might like to see if you could draw what coaching means to you. What images/ symbols come to you when you think of what coaching might be? What is your image?

Exercise

In whatever way suits you, illustrate: **What executive coaching means to me is...** *or you may prefer to answer the following series of questions.*

Thinking Through Executive Coaching

1. *What has been my experience of executive coaching to date?*
2. *What do I want from executive coaching?*
3. *What do I want from my executive coach?*
4. *What learning objectives would I like to bring to my coaching sessions?*
5. *What worries me about executive coaching?*
6. *Any worries about my executive coach?*
7. *What are the kinds of problems that could arise within executive coaching?*
8. *What interests me about executive coaching?*

Framework For Executive Coaching

...an overview of what executive coaching means...

To end this chapter, we thought we would include an overview of what executive coaching means. It's not ours but it very much contains what we too consider to be the "big picture" of executive coaching. For more details on each section, you will find reading the full chapter in Connor and Pokora (2007) helpful (chapter 1: What is effective coaching and mentoring?)

1. "The **learning relationship** is at the heart of change".
2. "The **context** is work".
3. "The **client** sets the agenda and is resourceful".
4. "The **coach** or **mentor** facilitates **Learning And Development**".
5. "The **outcome** is change".
6. "The **framework** for the change process provides movement and direction".
7. "The **skills** develop insight, release potential and deliver results".
8. "The **qualities** of the coach or mentor affirm, enable and sustain the client".
9. "The **ethical practice** safeguards and enhances coaching and mentoring".

(Connor and Pokora, 2007:7).

Conclusion

This chapter has provided an overview of executive coaching, of its purpose and more widely, its philosophy. We have made learning the rationale for coaching because we believe that learning equals change. Our hope is, as you end this chapter that you have come to an understanding of what executive coaching means to you and your role in it as a coachee.

Examples

Bernice has never had executive coaching before. Her Company has hired an Executive Coaching firm to provide executive coaching to her and her colleagues at this level of management. They are meeting together to discuss executive coaching with the HR Director. Bernice wonders how she can prepare for that meeting.

...James wonders how he can get out of this newfangled fad that will make his working life even more demanding...

James has heard that executive coaching will be provided for senior managers in his company. "Not again", he thinks, "why can't they leave us alone to get on with our jobs? This is another management tool to make sure we are up to scratch". James wonders how he can get out of this newfangled fad that will make his working life even more demanding.

Geraldine has been asked to meet with three potential executive coaches hired by her company. She is preparing to meet each in turn and wonders what she should ask each of them to get an idea of who might best work with her.

Review And Discussion

1. Outline your understanding of the essential elements in executive coaching. What does executive coaching mean for you?
2. Can you begin to articulate the characteristics of an effective executive coach?
3. How do you want to use executive coaching?
4. At this point in your development, what form of executive coaching would best suit you? (Look at the five areas above – knowledge, skills, qualities, learning from experience, learning how to learn, and transformational learning).
5. How does the context in which you work impact on your executive coaching?

Chapter 2

The Executive Coaching Relationship

Structuring Your Coaching Programme

To get your individual executive coaching programme up and running there will need to be a few structures put in place. These structures may or may not be of interest to you and you may, or may not be involved in them. However, for executive coaching to be most effective it is worth spending some time to ascertain whether or not these arrangements are in place in your company or organization. Executive coaching is a triadic relationship and all three players in the coaching game need to be given appropriate voices.

The structures or arrangements that are most important are:

1. Your organization's commitment and support for Executive Coaching.
2. Support from senior people in the organization.
3. Setting up a coaching culture.
4. Setting up a coaching structure within the organization.
5. Implementing executive coaching.
6. Evaluating Executive Coaching.

...check with your organization about what they do have set up to ensure the effective working of executive coaching...

This is the "big picture" or the landscape of executive coaching. The chances are you will be involved in No. 5: the stage of implementing executive coaching. However as Jarvis, Lane and Fillery-Travis (2006:10) point out: "Two thirds of organizations report that they do not have a formal strategy for their coaching activities." It may be that you will want to go back and check with your organization about what they do have set up to ensure the effective working of executive coaching. In the book quoted above (Jarvis, Lane and Fillery-Travis (2006), there is an excellent summary of lessons learned from people involved in the delivery and the management of coaching in organizational settings. They present 8 main areas with a number of factors in each: here we will simply present their eight areas and leave it to you investigate further if it is of interest to you. Their 8 areas are:

1. Build understanding and communicate.
2. Obtain buy-in.
3. Plan and Prepare.
4. Measure and demonstrate results.
5. Be selective (of coaches, coachees, developmental needs).
6. Take care over good selection (if external coaches).
7. Link with strategy and culture.
8. Provide training and support.

(pp. 73 – 76)

We are not going to consider most of these issues since they fall usually to senior managers and HR to consider and implement. However, we do not want to assume that all is well in your organization regarding your executive coaching. There is enough evidence from research to show that the infrastructure to ensure the success of executive coaching is not always in place eg., we know of instances where, in theory, time is given for executive coaching but in reality, coachees have to argue for it. Whybrow and Henderson (2007) have a comprehensive chapter entitled, "Concepts to support the integration and sustainability of coaching initiatives with Organizations", for those of you who might want to investigate some of these ideas further.

There is one area that will be of vital importance to you and your involvement in executive coaching that we will consider: setting up the coaching relationship and choosing your coach. The coachee-coach relationship is a vital component in effective executive coaching. O'Broin and Palmer (2007) summarize the elements which make change possible as a result of the relationship:

"Establishing and maintaining a strong working alliance, attempting to facilitate a high degree of collaboration, conducting the relationship in an empathetic way, being caring, warm and accepting, being congruent or authentic, resolving alliance ruptures in an empathetic way, noting that clients' expectations are likely to play a role in outcome" (p. 299).

This makes finding the right executive coach for you all the more important.

The Right Executive Coach For You

A good executive coaching relationship forms the basis of effective coaching. Little of significance will happen unless the relationships between the various people involved are healthy, contracted for, safe and trustworthy. These relationships involve:

1. The key relationship between executive coach and coachee.
2. The relationship between the executive coach and the company of which the coachee is an employee (we will look later at contracts as the basis of these relationships).

Hence, it is really important that you can work with your coach in a way that facilitates your learning. Research into executive coaching suggests that an effective coach demonstrates qualities such as empathy, acceptance, flexibility, openness with confrontation, a sense of humour and appropriate self-disclosure. Whether you have set up your executive coach's services yourself or whether that person has been chosen for you by someone else, remember that you are the consumer and that it is essential that your learning needs be adequately met in coaching. Remember also that your company is paying for executive coaching and will probably want to have a say in the agenda. Having said that, we are aware that some executive coaches and some organizations will not see executive coaching as a collaborative endeavour and it is easy to be labelled "difficult or demanding" when you try to negotiate a different concept of coaching. Trying to make executive coaching a collaborative alliance between all parties takes time and effort that is well worth spending.

...an executive coach who is too critical and challenging may leave you feeling unsupported...

Most coachees look to their executive coach to balance support with challenge so that they can benefit from new learning without feeling undermined in the process. A coach who is too accepting and supportive without also being appropriately challenging may leave you feeling uncertain about the quality of your work and about the challenging areas of your development. On the other hand, an executive coach who is too critical and challenging may leave you feeling unsupported, humiliated and inadequate. It is important to find in an executive coach the right balance between support and challenge and between positive feedback and constructive critical feedback so that you are helped to move forward in your work. You may find that this is a topic that you will want to raise at different times in your relationship with your coach. You will be keen to have an executive coach who works "with you" and not "on you" – you are hiring a coach not a counsellor or a psychotherapist and the relationships and roles and behaviours in these different interventions need to be clear.

Executive coaching is a unique relationship in that you and your coach will be discussing your professional development so you feel safe enough to be frank about your difficulties in order that you can derive the maximum benefit from the coaching process. Clear direct communication in coaching will enable you more easily to feed your learning back into your daily work. An executive coach with a good sense of humour can help to make the learning process a pleasure rather than a chore; humour that has a quality of sharing rather than shaming can often help us to recognize our foibles and our shortcomings without getting them out of proportion.

...two ways of choosing a coach: the formal competitive tender and the "scratch and sniff" method...

A short article entitled "The Frog Prince" (Moloney, 2005) talks of two ways of choosing a coach: the formal competitive tender and the "scratch and sniff" method. The author suggests a combination of the two and sees the stages for choosing your executive coach as comprising:

1. Trawling for names: getting recommendations: reviewing coach databases or in many instances in organizations the coaches will be chosen by HR or a senior executive either individually or by appointing a coaching organization.
2. Phoning potential coaches and asking the right questions: the kinds of questions asked at this initial stage will differ depending on needs. They may include questions about qualifications, experience, background, ethical codes etc.
3. Kissing the frog (meeting the individuals). If several individual executive coaches are short listed and meetings take place, then the coachee will be looking for appropriate style, connection with the coach, their ability to work together.
4. Deciding – the final decision is made and a working agreement (or contract) is drawn up (see Chapter 3).

Passmore and Gibbes (2007) surveyed the research literature on what are coachees' and executive coaches' perceptions of what they look for in suitable coaches. They present a table summarising the research of Hall, Otazo and Hollenbeck (1999).

What Works Best In Coaching?

From Coachees

1. Honest, realistic, challenging feedback.
2. Good listening.
3. Good action points ideas.
4. Clear objectives.
5. No personal agenda from coach.
6. Accessibility, availability.
7. Straight feedback.
8. Competence, sophistication.
9. Seeing a good model of effectiveness.
10. Coach has seen other career paths.

From Coaches

1. Connecting personally, recognising where the coachee is.
2. Good listening.
3. Reflecting.
4. Caring.
5. Learning.
6. Checking back.
7. Commitment to coachee success.
8. Demonstrating integrity.

9. Openness and honesty.
10. Knowing the unwritten rules.
11. Pushing the coachee where necessary.

Profile Of A Good Executive Coach

Jarvis (2004) outlines some characteristics of external coaches
that should be considered when making choices:

1. Appropriate level of coaching experience. The level of experience
   can be ascertained depending on factors such as: complexity of
   issues to be coached, the level of seniority of the coachee in the
   company, and prior experience of being an executive coach.
2. Relevant business/industry experience. Executive coaching takes place in an
   organizational setting and it would therefore be important that an external coach
   understand organizational dynamics and how to work with three way contracts.
3. References.
4. Background of the coach.
5. Supervision.
6. Breadth of tools, techniques and models used.
7. Understanding of boundaries and approach to referral.
8. Relevant qualifications and training.
9. Membership of appropriate bodies.
10. Professional indemnity insurance.
11. Other qualities/personal characteristics.

Jarvis (2004) also has a useful outline of the steps in the
process of selecting an individual coach:

1. Assess your development and professional needs.
2. Develop desired coach profile (individual and organizational).
3. Paper based selection to produce short list.
4. Meeting with individuals to assess.
5. Make selection and check with HR (or appropriate body).
6. Meet with Executive Coach to draw up working agreement
   (three way contract involving HR or manager).

Executive Coach Behaviours And Qualities

*...remember that
your executive
coach is human...*

Campbell (2000) has collected a list of qualities, characteristics, features and
behaviours of effective supervisors from literature, research and workshop
experiences. We think these same qualities apply to executive coaches. She presents
these in terms of behaviours and personal qualities: you might want to rate
your executive coach on these characteristics. As you do so, remember that your
executive coach is human: sometimes lists like the following can be a bit unrealistic
in expecting all executive coaches to have all these features all the time:

Effective executive coach behaviours.

He or she:

1. Clarifies expectations.
2. Shares his/her style of coaching.
3. Maintains consistent and appropriate boundaries.
4. Has knowledge of theory and current research.
5. Teaches practical skills.
6. Provides regular and scheduled coaching sessions.
7. Is accessible and available.
8. Encourages the exploration of new ideas and techniques.
9. Fosters autonomy.
10. Models appropriate ethical behaviour.
11. Is willing to act as a model.
12. Is personally and professionally mature.
13. Perceives growth as an ongoing process.
14. Is willing to assess the learning needs of executive coachees.
15. Provides constructive criticism and feedback.
16. Is invested in the development of the coachee.
17. Creates a relaxed learning environment.
18. Cares about the well-being of others.
19. Has the ability to be present and immediate.
20. Has an awareness of personal power.
21. Has the courage to expose vulnerabilities, make mistakes, and take risks.
22. Is nonauthoritarian and nonthreatening.
23. Accepts and celebrates diversity.
24. Has the ability to communicate effectively.
25. Is willing to engage in a number of learning formats (imagination etc).
26. Is aware of, and accepts, own limitations and strengths.
27. Is willing to negotiate.
28. Works collaboratively.

Personal Qualities and Characteristics.

He or she will have:

1. A sense of humour.
2. Integrity.
3. People-orientation.
4. Trustworthiness.
5. Honesty.
6. Tenaciousness.
7. Openness and flexibility.
8. Competency.
9. Credibility.
10. Considerateness.
11. Respectfulness.
12. Understanding.
13. Sensitivity.
14. Objectivity.
15. Congruence.
16. Tactfulness.
17. Genuineness.
18. Curiosity.
19. Intelligence.
20. Warmth.
21. Supportiveness.

...the courage to expose vulnerabilities, make mistakes, and take risks...

22 Tolerance.

23 Encouragement.

24 Availability.

If you would like to pursue this further then we suggest you look at Law, Ireland and Hussain (2007): page 77 summarizes the qualities and skills needed by successful mentors/coaches.

There is always the tendency to expect that the ideal executive coach is just around the corner. While the list above is pretty long and exhaustive it is unlikely, this side of heaven, to find an executive coach that fulfils all these characteristics and engages in all of these behaviours. Executive coaches are human beings and many of them are learning (and still learning) how to be effective.

...Beware the psychological contract as you begin your search for the executive coach...

Beware the psychological contract as you begin your search for the executive coach who will accompany you on your professional development. The psychological contract is the unhidden and unwritten set of expectations you bring to relationships (see Chapter 3). Sometimes those expectations are wildly unrealistic and impossible for anyone to meet. It might be worthwhile (with pen and paper) outlining your expectations from an executive coach.

Exercise

On paper write down everything you can think of that you would like from your executive coach (don't monitor this closely and don't worry about how idealistic or unrealistic you might be).

When you have done this, go through your expectations and mark them in one of three ways:

1. *This is a realistic and realisable feature of an executive coach*
2. *This is a realistic feature but would only come with experience and time or*
3. *These expectations are unrealistic and I cannot expect them in an executive coach (eg., having all the answers, will always be available to me, will have "been there" and know how to tackle the problems I bring, will never cause me conflict).*

Interviewing A Prospective Executive Coach

At times coachees have the option of choosing their executive coach. If this is the case then we suggest that you spend time ensuring you have the best executive coach for you. You will want to meet with at least one possible contender for the job, possibly more.

When meeting prospective executive coaches, it is a good idea to have some questions ready:

1. What are your qualifications and experience in executive coaching?
2. To which professional bodies are you affiliated?
3. To what Code of Ethics for Executive Coaches do you subscribe? Can I have a copy of it?
4. What is the principal orientation in your work? Have you any theoretical base or model from which you work?
5. What is the central tenet of your coaching philosophy?

6. Do you have experience of working with similar people to myself or with similar organizations?
7. How will you expect me to prepare for my coaching session with you? What information will you need in advance? And what information do you want me to bring to each session?
8. Will we be able to vary our activities in the coaching sessions?
9. What are your current interests in my field?
10. Can I see an example of your executive coaching contract?
11. Will we have regular reviews of my progress and of our work together?
12. How do you give constructive feedback?
13. How will we contract together with my manager (sponsor) to ensure we subscribe to the same goals?
14. How do you support your own development and learning?

Questions for yourself after meeting a prospective executive coach:

1. Did I feel relaxed and at ease with this person?
2. Did I have a sense that I could learn from this person?
3. Does this person possess a body of knowledge that is of interest and potential use to me?
4. Did I leave with a respect for this person's experience in the field?
5. Was I able to be honest and open with this person?
6. Did I feel satisfied with the answers to my questions?
7. Did this person have a sense of humour that I responded to positively?
8. Did I get a sense that I would receive honest feedback, both about my strengths and my areas of growth in an atmosphere of acceptance?
9. Did the person answer my questions in an open, nondefensive manner?

...Professional coaches will not be insulted or hurt if you opt not to work with them...

Professional coaches will not be insulted or hurt if you opt not to work with them. They understand very well that there are a range of reasons why a coachee might want to and might not want to choose them as their coach. It is always helpful if coachees can say why they have chosen to work with someone else but it is not necessary to do so. If the executive coach does not understand that then it is probably a sign that you have made a good choice.

When you are not in a position to choose your own executive coach, you may still ask yourself the same questions and perhaps make these a basis for negotiation where possible. For example, you could request straight and honest feedback about both your strengths and weaknesses in the course of coaching. And you can ask for a reciprocal contract that allows you to give feedback about what has been useful to you and what is less useful in coaching. In this way you can set the scene for the building of a good working alliance and capitalize on what this particular professional can offer you. It is also good to ask what are the person's areas of particular interest so that you can benefit from these.

You may not have an immediate answer to some of these questions; it may be an idea to see if you can negotiate to have a trial period of say, six sessions in which you can get to know one another and assess if the coaching alliance is working well.

Remember that research (into helping interventions such as supervision, counselling and psychotherapy) regularly suggests that it is the quality of the working alliance that most contributes to the effectiveness of the outcome. You need a space where you know you can bring your real concerns and where you will receive honest feedback and help. The kind of response an executive coach will want to hear is one that came from a small group of coachees who said: "We know that you will be honest with us about our mistakes, so for that reason we really value your positive feedback too. You are not just trying to make us feel good! When we get negative feedback, it is delivered in such a way that we can hear it and we do not feel shamed or put down. If we are unsure about something it is safe to ask you to explain. It is as though it is OK to make mistakes because that is how everyone learns." This response reflects a balance between appropriate support and caring confrontation and points to a good working alliance.

As mentioned above, there are times when executive coachees have no say in the choice of their coach. Executive coaches are appointed because of contracts with coaching organizations and practicalities in allocating coachees to coaches. While this may not be a problem and may not affect the quality of the relationship or the coaching itself, it is worth taking time to look at possible implications. Sue Kaberry (1995) researched the area of abuse in supervision and interviewed 14 supervisees who claimed that their supervision was abusive in one form or another. Interestingly, 9 out of the 14 interviewees had been appointed their supervisor. While this is not necessarily the same in executive coaching, there is some credence in the belief that if I choose to work with someone (rather than have that person chosen for me) then I will be more motivated and more easily invested in the outcomes.

We recommend that when you have been allocated an executive coach you have not chosen for yourself that you:

1. Talk about the fact that you have not chosen one another and review what it means for each of you. Executive coaches too, at times, have strong feelings about this method of setting up executive coaching arrangements and may need to talk about their reactions to it.
2. Look at the possible implications of this arrangement for your work together. Where executive coaches sometimes have to engage in coaching as part of their overall job, they may approach the task with resentment or lack of enthusiasm or energy. Coachees, on the other hand, can see their lack of choice as giving permission not to participate in coaching (one of us had such a coachee who considered it was his right to be there, as required, but to expect the executive coach to guide and give direction and provide the answers without his active participation).
3. Schedule in review times to ensure that there are no negative practices enter the coaching arena as a result of being appointed an executive coach.
4. Be specific about the expectations of each other in coaching and clear about expectations from respective organizations (the psychological contract mentioned above).

This type of arrangement in executive coaching is akin to an arranged marriage, where couples give their consent but may have little say in the choice of their partner. There is no reason why it may not work if both parties are prepared to talk openly about their feelings and work towards an agreed coaching arrangement. Starting with the expectation that it will work is often a good beginning.

Codes Of Ethics And Professional Bodies

We would expect all executive coaches to belong to an appropriate professional body (such as BPS, APECS, EMCC, ICF, CIPD) and in turn subscribe to an Ethical Framework or a Code of Ethics and Practice for Coaches. Executive coaches will not be hurt or insulted if you ask them to let you know about both of these – their Professional Body and their Code of Ethics. Many coaches make their Code of

Ethics available to coachees. If you wanted to look at sample Codes of Ethics then you can view them at the web sites of the Professional Bodies, eg., www.emccouncil. org and www.apeccs.org. In Appendix 18 we have put a recent joint statement from four of the main professional bodies concerned with Coaching around best ethical practice. You might want to have a look at that appendix before moving on.

Conclusion

...We have also highlighted the importance of your particular relationship with your executive coach...

In Chapter 2, we have emphasized the importance your organization plays in helping you set up your coaching relationship and particularly in providing the culture and environment to support it. We have also highlighted the importance of your particular relationship with your executive coach. That relationship will make or break executive coaching for you. It cannot be stressed enough how important it is that you find the person best suited to facilitate your learning. Time spent on that choice is time well spent.

Example

Ferdi was last in line when the "beauty parade" took place and by the time his choice came around there was only one space left, in effect no choice. He was a bit envious that his fellow directors had had some say in who would be their executive coach and he had particularly wanted to work with Geoff. Naturally Geoff's two slots were quickly filled. Ferdi would have to work with Damian. He was not impressed with the mechanism for being with Damian. He knew he was resentful when he arrived for his first meeting.

Review And Discussion

1. What, in your view, are the characteristics of an effective executive coach and one you would like to work with?
2. Are you in a position to choose who will be your executive coach (even if you are appointed one)? How do you feel about that and how might it impact on your working together?
3. How would you know if the coaching relationship was deteriorating or being less helpful than you would want?
4. How might you handle the situation if you felt the coaching relationship was deteriorating?
5. What are your expectations from executive coaching and which of these are a) realistic b) unrealistic?

Chapter 3

The Executive Coaching Contract

Introduction And Overview

The executive coaching partnership involved a number of stakeholders. To be effective all need to agree to, be clear about and subscribe to the same objectives. The Executive Coaching Handbook (2004) captures this well: "The coaching partnership is a win-win approach in which all the partners plan the process together, communicate openly, and work cooperatively toward the ultimate accomplishment of overarching organizational objectives" (page 21). Part of that planning is contracting together.

Contracts (overt and covert) underpin all relationships whether these are one-to-one, team or organizational. They contain the agreements, conscious and unconscious, of all parties in the relationship and the rules and procedures that guide these relationships. Overall, contracts revolve around:

1. "Exchange" (what we will do for each other).
2. A sense of "reciprocity" (two/multi- way arrangements).
3. "Choice" (I or we freely enter this arrangement).
4. Some sense of "predictability" (we can have some guarantees that this will happen).
5. The future (we "will" do).
6. The responsibilities of parties concerned (I will take accountability for doing x if you take accountability for doing y).
7. Regular reviews.

...The psychological contract is the subjective side that contains our hidden agendas...

While overt contracts attempt to articulate these elements, either verbally or in written form, words and gestures are always open to interpretation. It is because they are open to interpretation that a "psychological contract" is part of all contracts. Individuals bring to their contracts and agreements their own assumptions, beliefs and expectations most of which will be unspoken and unnegotiated. The psychological contract is the subjective side that contains our hidden agendas. This chapter will look at the importance of both types of contracts, the overt and the covert, in executive coaching.

Our suggestion is that you have clear and focused contracts that articulate the roles and responsibilities of all the parties involved in the executive coaching arrangement. We use the plural here "contracts" because in most coaching arrangements there will be a number of contracts and as the central figure of executive coaching you, the coachee, will be involved in more than one of them.

Let us look at the possible "big picture" of executive coaching. Your company or organization may have hired (contracted with) an executive coaching company to provide coaches to engage in individual coaching sessions with executives in your company. Look at the number of possible relationships involved (See Figure 3.1):

You may add further relationships to this already complex arrangement eg. a supervisor who works with the Executive coach and is hired by the Coaching Organization.

Example

Let us look at a possible example to see the kinds of relationships involved and therefore the possible contracts needed if all are to "sing from the same hymn-sheet" and be clear and in agreement at what is happening at every stage of the executive coaching arrangements.

George is a professional and experienced executive coach who works as an associate for a coaching company called ExCoach Supreme. He sees executives from an organization called AVEC. AVEC have contracted with ExCoach Supreme for 50 of its executives to have ongoing executive coaching for six months. It is part of George's contact with ExCoach Supreme that he engages in supervision for his work and this is provided by ExCoach Supreme in a small group of three executive coaches and a supervisor who is external to ExCoach Supreme. George's supervisor provides an annual supervisor report to ExCoach Supreme and would contact the Coaching Manager if she had reservations about the work that George was doing. Otherwise, overall she has no other contact with anyone in the executive coaching system other than George. There is also a Coaching Manager, an employee of ExCoach Supreme, who oversees coaching cases and who will contact George (or indeed, George will contact her) if there are any administrative or coaching decisions to be made regarding coachees (eg., request for more coaching sessions over and above their allocated lot of six months, where there is the need for referral as in the case of alcohol or drug abuse, or where there are crisis issues eg., such as is a suicidal coachee or one who needs ongoing psychotherapy). Imagine the relationships, contracts and psychological contracts at work when a coachee (let's call her Mandy) comes to George from the Company through the Coaching Manager for executive coaching.

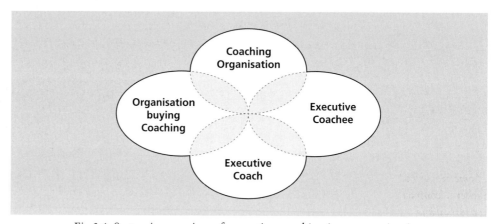

Fig 3.1: Systemic overview of executive coaching in an organization.

There are eight overt contracts (See Figure 3.2):

1. The employment contract between George and ExCoach Supreme.
2. The coaching contract between George and Mandy.
3. The supervision contract between George and his Supervisor.
4. The contract between George's supervisor and ExCoach Supreme.
5. The coaching management contract between George and the Coaching manager from ExCoach Supreme.
6. The contract between the Coaching manager and ExCoach Supreme.
7. The contract between ExCoach Supreme and Mandy's Company.
8. The employment contract between the Company and the individual employee who is coming for executive coaching (in this instance, Mandy).

...alive with unseen but active psychological contracts...

While there are eight overt and probably written contracts, there is double that amount of psychological contracts (16) present in the above set of relationships. So while George and ExCoach Supreme have a written contract both have signed, each will have a very different psychological contract with one another. This executive coaching room is alive with unseen but active psychological contracts and awash with the implications of these 16 psychological contracts at work at different levels of the system. How easy it is for different expectations to arise, for roles to be unclear, for information to pass unwittingly (and outside confidentiality) through different parts of the system and for unethical and unprofessional issues to emerge.

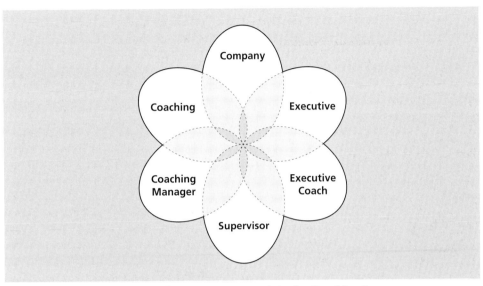

Figure 3.2: Eight Contracts at work in the Coaching System.

We define the coaching contract as a working agreement between executive coach, coachee(s) and their company/organization. In executive coaching, as we have seen from the above this contract is at least three-way. Just as executive coaching is a triadic relationship, so executive coaching contracts are at least triadic.

...Some people find the term 'contract' too formal and prefer terms like 'goal'...

Some people find the term 'contract' too formal and prefer terms like 'goal' or 'focus'. Others use the term "working agreements". We are not highly invested in using the word "contract" and in some settings it will the entirely wrong word to use. Think of what might be the best word in your context to capture that sense of agreement between all parties. What we are looking for are clear, focused agreements to which the participants agree and adhere. In this way we work together and we know what we can expect from ourselves and each other. Hopefully, the whole system is in harmony.

Contracts can be made to establish a focus for an individual session or for a longer term, say to outline the overall goals for four to six sessions or, even in some cases, for six months or for a year. We see a benefit to both types of contracting. The longer-term contract provides an overall focus to the work, and the session-by-session contract provides an agreed focus for an individual session.

Contracts work best if they are specific and have well-defined outcomes. Examples are:

"I want to focus on my relationship with my team so that I am more assertive in making clear what my expectations are of people and so I do not end up angry and resentful at the end of each day."

OR

"What I want to do in this session is discuss the presentation that I am planning to do to verify that the ideas flow logically together and see if the sequencing and logical connection between ideas is fine. I also want to check that I am not striving to cover too much."

Contracting In Executive Coaching

You and your coach will negotiate the contract to ensure that it is not too ambitious for the time available. Contracts are most effective if they list clear behavioural outcomes that you wish to achieve by the end of the coaching. These outcomes need to be realistic within the time-frame and relate to behaviours, feelings and thoughts that you can change and which are within your control. Contracts are not about changing other people, however much we may want that!

...Contracts differ and here we describe briefly the different types...

Contracts differ and here we describe briefly the different types of contracts that may be involved in the contracting process.

Two-Way Contracts

(See Appendices 2, 3 and 4 for examples). A simple two-way contract is made between the coachee and the coach and is a private arrangement between them although it will often be made within the context of a broader contract with the Company. The essence of this agreement is that the coachee will bring his/her work to the coach who will provide the time and place for reflection and learning.

Three Way Contracts

These contracts are three-cornered in that the agreement involves three parties: the coachee, the coach and the organization. In these cases it is the organization that both pays for the coaching and is an important 'third party' in the agreement. Contracts may differ in the degree of contact between the coach and the organization: generally, however, the coach will agree to make some form of report to the organization, the confidentiality boundaries of which needs to be clearly stipulated and understood by all three parties before the contracted work begins.

Four Way Contracts

Jarvis et al (2006: 35) includes line mangers in the four-way contract outlined in their book. The four participants in this contract are: executive coach, executive coachee, the organization and the line-manager of the coachee. In our view this is an important addition since line managers traditionally may have little to do with the coaching processes taking place. A recent doctoral dissertation (Grace-Roland, 2008) has called line managers "invisible" when it comes to their part in mentoring/coaching programmes and, while not necessarily against the process, do not feel that they should or ought to be involved. Contracts involving line managers work best when they make clear their roles and responsibilities within the overall process rather than leaving it to chance and to individual "taste" whether or not they get involved.

The Business Contract

Refers to the practicalities of the agreement eg. times, venue (often this will be at the place of work), length of meetings, how payments will take place and with what frequency (after each session or at the end of a stipulated period), to whom the invoice will be addressed and sent, cancellation agreements, limits of confidentiality, information details required by the coach, copies of forms to be filled out, etc. This is the administrative aspect of the agreement. The limits of confidentiality with regards to feedback to the organization need to be carefully considered in terms of what information is given and to whom this is addressed so that you, as coachee, are clear about this from the start.

The Psychological Contract

Refers to the agreement (on a more implicit level) where the coach is committed to co-creating with the coachee an environment where the coachee feels at ease and is able to discuss sensitive issues with a coach who will not judge them. It is at this level that problems often arise since the coach and the coachee may have very different expectations of the process of coaching and if these are not clearly articulated and thrashed out, then misunderstandings and disappointments may arise. If there is any hidden agenda on the part of the coach, the coachee or the organization that has not been openly admitted or revealed at the outset, this agenda may well undermine the effectiveness of the coaching process and can in turn lead to 'games' and 'ruptures' in the coaching alliance. We would, therefore, encourage you at the outset to discuss very carefully your expectations of coaching and establish clarity of purpose. We trust that this booklet will help you in that process. We have a section in Chapter 12 around "critical moments" in executive coaching which inevitably bring up issues around trust in the coaching relationship. You might want to have a look at that section just now as a way of anticipating possible conflicts.

Managing The Psychological Contract

It is often the difficulties within the psychological contract that result in formal and informal complaints, legal stances and breakdowns in professional (and indeed personal) relationships. It is imperative to look at how executive coaches and executive coachees can anticipate and work with this side of the contract to avoid such happenings.

Hewson (1999) has suggested ideas on managing the psychological contract in a healthy manner:

1. All parties are involved actively in developing the contract.
2. The contract provides a mental set or overall perception of what end goal is in mind for everyone.
3. Contracting creates a guard against the abuse of power and all participants are aware of and patrol the boundaries of power.
4. Overt contracts are designed to minimize covert agendas.
5. Transparency, honesty, openness and dialogue are built into contracting.
6. Contracts are often developmental (they change and need to change over time eg., as in marriage) and need to be re-negotiated. The psychological contract is part of that development..
7. Contracts are emotional arenas as well as rational agreements.
8. Pay heed to the social, political, organizational and professional contexts in which contracts are lived and played out.
9. Pick up subtle shifts in expectations from those who are part of the contract – articulate these expectations.
10. Track the relationships to see if any new needs emerge (eg., that the coachee might need more support or counselling).

Contracts have been compared by Proctor (2000) to Russian Dolls. There are contracts within contacts and can take place between different parties within the overall coaching system:

There is the overall contract between the two companies

1. Within that is the contract between the individual coach and the Coaching Company.
2. Within that there is the executive coaching contract between the executive coach and the executive coachee.
3. These, and the other contracts, need to be aligned so that all are agreed on what will happen.

Within the context of the above agreements, you will then also contract session-by-session regarding your needs and goals for that particular session. These sessional contracts will help you to keep focused on your learning needs. It is important then that you spell your needs out clearly and concisely at the outset of each session.

...this way means that you and your coach can keep track of your goals in an ongoing way and not get sidetracked...

Contracting can also be used as a relational tool within the session so that you can make mini-contracts when you want more or less of something or when a need or area of interest arises in the course of a session and you want to change direction. An example of such a mini-contract is a manager who realizes he is very good at supporting his team but quite poor at challenging negative behaviour. Within the session he and the executive coach draw up a mini contract to support him being more challenging. Using contracting in this way means that you and your coach can keep track of your goals in an ongoing way and not get sidetracked into something that is not of use to you.

Connor and Pokora (2007) list a number of items which they suggest considering as part of a working agreement.

"Practical"

1. "Having a pre-coaching or mentoring introductory session"
2. "Agreeing location – where will you meet?"
3. "Frequency – how often will you meeting? Minimum/maximum number of sessions"
4. "Length of session – what would you prefer? Agree to?"
5. "Payment – how much? Payment procedure?"
6. "Cancellation – policy for missed session? What if the client is late?"

"Working Relationship"

1. "Preferred ways of working together"
2. "Tools and techniques you might use"
3. "Your values and the learning relationship"
4. "Balance of support and challenge you might offer"
5. "Feedback – 360 degree, other?"
6. "How clients learn best?"
7. "Framework or model you use"
8. "Your expectations – work outside of sessions"

"Professional"

1. "Your qualifications"

2. "Your experience/references"
3. "Your responsibilities: legal, to the sponsor, to your profession or organization"
4. "Any possible conflicts of interest?"
5. "Note-taking: who takes? Who keeps? For how long?"
6. "Supervision – your arrangements"

"Ethical"

1. "An explicit working agreement"
2. "Built-in ongoing review"
3. "Confidentiality: extent and limits"
4. "Clear role boundaries"
5. "Ending session

(Connor and Pokora, 2007: 32).

Appendix 15 is worth reviewing just now. It is a format that our friend, John Nixon, gives to his new coachees to help them prepare for their first coaching session.

Managing Confidentiality

...Steps need to be taken, before executive coaching begins, to set up a confidentiality structure...

A crucial part of the executive coaching partnership, and an essential ingredient in all the above contracts, is an agreed understanding of what "confidentiality" means to all parties concerned. When it is not clear (and unfortunately at times even when it has been agreed) leakage of information can take place when so many players are concerned: the organization, the managers, HR, the coaching company, the individual's executive coach, the executive himself or herself and other stakeholders or participants. Steps need to be taken, before executive coaching begins, to set up a confidentiality structure so that all stakeholders are clear about what is agreed.

There are four types of confidentiality and it is firstly important to know which type is being considered in executive coaching and not assume there is automatic agreement on what confidentiality means. The four types are:

1. Absolute confidentiality is an agreement where under no circumstances would confidentiality be broken no matter what information was discussed or revealed. The most obvious example of absolute confidentiality is the Roman Catholic confessional. It would also seem to pertain for solicitors and barristers who have "privileged information". Often coachees think that absolute confidentiality is being offered when it is not but because of lack of clarity they can get upset and angry if disclosure needs to take place with or without their permission.
2. Limited Confidentiality agrees that what is discussed and shared between parties will be confidential with agreed exceptions to that rule, eg., one of us worked with an oil company where knowledge of alcohol or drug abuse on the oil rigs had to be fed back to the Company. It was written into the agreement and all parties were aware of it. Other common instances of limited confidentiality are: where there is serious danger to self or others, or child abuse and other harmful activities. However, please note that all citizens in the United Kingdom are legally bound to disclose confidential information if it involves terrorism or drug money laundering. What is excluded from being confidential varies in relation to the context but what is important is that all parties are aware of these conditions and agree to them before coaching commences.

...start with a blank sheet of paper and work out the type of confidentially that best suits them...

3. Discretionary confidentiality is where coachees or clients leave it to the discretion of the coach where and when to use the information that emerges from their coaching sessions. This is a very trusting attitude; this model worked well in a situation where one of us ran a youth counselling service in London. Many young people (not all indeed) would give the counsellor permission to use whatever they needed in the welfare and help of the young person himself or herself.

4. Negotiated confidentiality is a form of confidentially that can cover any or all of the above (and will pertain in all situations) but where the participants start with a blank sheet of paper and work out the type of confidentially that best suits them. This will involve discussions with and about how to involve/or not, other stakeholders in the coaching arrangement. However, the negotiation will also reflect individual needs and circumstances. For example, one of us worked with coachee on a private basis who asked that she remain anonymous as part of the confidentiality (the rationale given for this was that her husband was very well known and she could not take the risk of anything being known about him).

Our suggestion is that the norm in Executive Coaching will be "limited confidentiality" where it will be clear about where and when and to whom disclosures are made.

The Executive Coaching Handbook (2004) presents a good method and approach to managing confidentiality:

"The executive and other members of the organization must be able to open up and share information with the coach and one another without fear hat the information will be passed on inappropriately or without their approval. Because each coaching situation is unique, it is important for all partners to develop a formal, written confidentiality agreement before the coaching begins. This agreement specifies what information will and will not be shared, in which circumstances, with whom, and how. The agreement helps all coaching partners remain sensitive to confidentiality issues from each others' points of view. Coaching partners should communicate with others members of the partnership before sharing any information with anyone outside the partnership" (page 45).

Exercise

Look at the executive coaching contracts in Appendices 2, 3 and 4 and see if what they say about confidentiality helps you feel safe as a coachee. Is there anything you would change about the wording? Is there anything you would add to what is here? Or take away? Could you write your own summary of what kind of confidentiality would best help you be safe and transparent and trusting in your coaching partnership?

Conclusion

From a contractual point of view, executive coaching is a complicated hall of mirrors. When multiple contracts (as in the case of executive coaching) are aligned and connected, then smooth running and agreed ways of working can be seen and implemented. When not aligned, then problems emerge, psychological games are played and executive coaching descends into battles over agreements and territories. Learning is high-jacked by administration and ends up in disharmony.

Examples

Jim arrives for his executive coaching session and suggests to his coach that today they work on his major presentation to the Board in a week's time. Jim wants this to go particularly well since it will be his best platform for influencing his ambitions to become MD. The coaching contract they drew up with the current MD and HR does not include this but focuses on two goals: his ability to delegate and his skills in mentoring his direct reports. Jill, his coach is anxious that he is using coaching to further his own career and that her contract is about other areas of his development.

...He was concerned that he seemed unable to establish a confident 'adult' relationship with his boss...

Jack arrived for coaching having requested a coach primarily to help him in his relationship with his boss. He was concerned that he seemed unable to establish a confident 'adult' relationship with his boss and tended to feel 'small and silly when I talk to him'. What I want is to say clearly what I think and also to feel at ease to 'just chat a bit" when that seems appropriate. Our relationship is very formal and stilted and that does not make for easy contact'. The coach agreed to work with Jim on establishing clear, straightforward adult communication with his boss. This was achieved by looking at some of Jim's beliefs that stood in his way when he approached his boss. In the discussion, Jim revealed that he had been bullied at school and remained 'very scared of the big boys'. Helping Jim separate his boss from 'those boys' in his mind and talk openly with his boss formed the heart of the coaching contract. He ceased feeling 'small and silly' and was able to relate in a more effective manner.

Review And Discussion

1. What are the features of an effective contract?
2. Do you think you are now able to negotiate a coaching contract with your coach?
3. What might you do if your coach is not interested in negotiating clear confidentiality boundaries between the two of you and the organization?
4. What part will the psychological contract play in your overall contract with your coach? With the organization?
5. How would you judge whether you have made an effective contract with your coach?

Chapter 4

The Executive Coaching Conversation

Outline Of The Coaching Conversation

...Executive coaching is based on a particular type of conversation...

It may seem obvious to say that the conversation between executive coach and executive coachee is at the centre of executive coaching. Executive coaching is based on a particular type of conversation. We suggest that that conversation is primarily one of dialogue.

It is **not**:

1. Monologue – where one or other of the parties dictates to the other.
2. Debate – where we intellectually compete to win.
3. Discussion – where we discuss possibilities.
4. Negotiation – where we work out possibilities together from a position of difference.
5. Conflict management – where we resolve differences.

Elements of all of the above will find their way into the coaching conversation at times – however none of them is executive coaching. Executive coaching conversations are characterized by:

1. Their focus – it is on the performance and potential of the coachee.
2. Their relationship – it is on collaboration and learning together.
3. Their talk – it is dialogue.

Their content: it is about the coachee's relationship and performance to their work and to their organization.

At this stage, if you want to look in more detail at dialogue as a form of conversation and communication, then go to Chapter 6 and read the section on Learning how to Dialogue. Other readings that might help here are:

1. Fierce Conversation: Achieving Success at Work and in Life; One Conversation at a Time (Susan Scott, 2002)
2. Difficult Conversations: What to Say in Tricky Situations without Ruining your Relationship (Ann Dickson, 2004)
3. Difficult Conversations: How to discuss what matters most (Stone, Patton and Heen, 2000)

Some questions on the executive coaching conversation:

1. What do we not talk about in Executive Coaching – why not?
2. Does our talk stress deficiency or growth (strengths)?
3. What are the conversations that are safe for us to have, what are the conversations we are anxious about having?

A more detailed and difficult set of questions are:

1. What voices need to be heard?
2. What words need to be spoken?
3. What truth needs to be acknowledged?
4. What connections need to be made?
5. What assumptions need to be challenged?
6. What beliefs need to be reviewed?
7. What emotions need to be expressed?
8. What actions need to be taken?

9. What relationships need to be named?
10. What secrets need to be uncovered?
11. What strengths need to be seen?
12. What limitations need to be articulated?
13. What successes need to be celebrated?
14. What losses need to be grieved?
15. What mental maps need to be surfaced?
16. What is the shift/development movement that needs to be enabled?

In summary, there are a number of stages in the coaching conversation:

1. Psychological preparation for the Executive Coaching conversation – what is permissible to bring to coaching?
2. Preparing for coaching: longer term and immediately
3. Knowing your learning objectives
4. Presenting in coaching
5. Keeping notes of coaching sessions
6. Evaluating the coaching session

We will look at each of these in turn.

Preparation For Coaching

...improving your 'emotional intelligence' in the interests of improving your skills as an executive...

Coaching covers areas related to your workplace. These may range from dealing with a challenge you are facing with a colleague, to getting help with management skills, or improving your 'emotional intelligence' in the interests of improving your skills as an executive, to supporting you in a promotion that you have recently received.

When we speak to new coachees about what to bring to coaching we say that coaching is about any issue that impinges on your working life and may be causing you difficulties at present in your work. However, the primary focus remains on your performance in the workplace, though some of the particular subject matter may be more personal.

There are a number of ways in which you can find out what would be most helpful for you to bring to coaching. We may not always be aware of our areas for development. Feedback from others (360 Degree feedback, Appraisal feedback and more informal feedback) may well suggest the agenda for executive coaching. It may be that your company or organization has already named some areas it would like you to focus on.

Examples

Esme is a HR Director and has a good reputation for getting work done and being in control and in charge of her team. A throw-away remark by her secretary (said lightly) made her think – "I notice how difficult it is for you to receive negative feedback". She had never quite allowed this into her consciousness before: it suddenly hit her when Mary said it off the cuff. She asked about this in an easy way amongst her colleagues and the general agreement was that most did not give her negative feedback because they sensed it upset her greatly. She has decided to make this the focus of her next coaching conversation.

Edward is about to begin his executive coaching arrangement. Before doing so he meets with the HR Director (Esme above). She tells him that the general consensus is that he is on the way to the Board and that overall, the Company wants to keep him and invest in his abilities. She suggests that one area that will help him enormously will be building up his ability to delegate. Feedback suggests that he is still wary about giving responsibility to others and delegating some of his own work to direct reports (which he could easily do). Esme says she will be communicating this developmental need to Edward's coach so that they can work on it together.

Preparing For Coaching

Preparing carefully for coaching is one of the best "insurance policies" for it working well. Effective preparation entails having a clear method of preparation and a way of ensuring that you bring to coaching what you most need to learn. Some areas worth reviewing are:

1. Do I have clear goals for coaching or am I uncertain about what exactly would be appropriate?
2. Am I inclined to bring only my problems to coaching and not mention my strengths?
3. Am I aware that there are aspects of my work that I would prefer not to bring to coaching?
4. Do I carefully edit what I bring to coaching in order to avoid potential or feared shame and embarrassment?
5. Do I prepare in advance for the coaching session, to ensure that I make good use of it?

...Preparation is the "before" of coaching, the time spent when I think through, reflect on, sift and decide on my agenda...

Answers to these questions will help you think through openly and honestly about how you prepare for coaching. Preparation is the "before" of coaching, the time spent when I think through, reflect on, sift and decide on my agenda. Some requirements for being able to do this are:

1. Time set aside for preparation.
2. Creating an environment of reflection, honesty and openness with oneself.
3. Recall of work (using your notes from your work).
4. Creating an agenda (prioritizing).

Here are some methods you could use to help your preparation:

1. Process Recordings of meetings giving the key interactions and decisional points: after the meeting you write out as fully as possible as much as you can remember of the dialogue and discussion.
2. Team preparation/small group preparation.
3. Keeping a 'learning journal' in which you can record your observations and reflections.

When you have identified a situation/ issue you wish to focus on in coaching, you can begin to ask yourself the following questions to clarify your enquiry:

1. What do I think about the situation? (Your 'thinking map' of the situation).
2. What is going on in the situation? (Observing the process of interaction between people).
3. What information is lacking in the situation? (Vital information may be lacking that would change your perception of events).

4. What to do I need to do about the situation? (The 'how to's': decide on practical behavioural steps to take you forward). (Clarkson and Gilbert, 1991).

Working out practical strategies to implement in the work situation is central to effective coaching. Arriving at these strategies will be helped by considering the first three questions in the process of the analysis.

Knowing Your Learning Objectives

...it is worth focusing on what you want from the session...

As you prepare for your executive coaching session and organize your agenda it is worth focusing on what you want from the session. One way is to see if you can distinguish between the following:

1. A puzzle - something I can resolve that is confusing to me just now and for which there is an answer that would apply to most situations and people eg., how to answer the phone in a more facilitative manner. A puzzle has one right answer.
2. A problem: again what is solvable but the solution will change from person to person and from situation to situation eg., my relationship with my boss. There is an answer to a problem but each person has to find his or her own particular answer.
3. A paradox: something that cannot be solved but with which I have to learn to live eg., that I am going to be made redundant and would prefer not to be; that my father has died and I am not sure how I can live without him.
4. A psychological problem: a problem that keeps recurring eg., all my relationships with my male bosses end up in fights. This is a recurring and repetitive pattern.
5. A mystery: events that happen in life that are difficult or impossible for me to make sense of eg., why do I have cancer when I have done nothing wrong to deserve it; if there a God how does he allow suffering; why must we die etc.

Each of the above needs a different intervention to resolve it: hence the importance of knowing what you are dealing with.

Exercise

Preparing for coaching

Have your notebook beside you. Relax, take some deep breaths and allow yourself to concentrate on your breathing for a minute or two. Then let your mind drift back over your recent work.

What surfaces for you immediately? Notice it and let it go (you might want to make a note of it in your notebook). Let your mind wander over the following questions:

1. *What interactions/situations/achievements were you pleased with?*
2. *What was difficult for you?*
3. *What were you/ are you, uncertain about?*
4. *What are you looking forward to in your next working session?*
5. *Are there any anxieties about the way you are working with a particular situation?*
6. *Are there any anxieties about your relationship with clients/managers/team members etc?*
7. *Are there some doubts/anxieties/feelings just "out of view" which you would rather keep out of view? Identify the feelings as well as the items.*

48

8. *What interactions have you enjoyed most at work? What were the feelings?*

Jot down a list of what has surfaced for you as a result of this reverie.

Scan though your records/notes: do any further points stand out for you, which you would like/need to talk about? Add to your list.

Imagine you are replaying a video of one session (or part of one): are there any ideas or feelings, which come up for you which you, might, or might not, like to bring to your coach? Note them.

Read through your list. Mark with an N any items which do not seem significant enough to bring to coaching just now, mark with a P any items you feel reluctant to talk about and would rather postpone (there may not be any). Tentatively prioritize the remaining items by numbering Item, 1, 2, 3 etc.

If you have marked some P items, gently explore with yourself: what are the actual or imagined risks to you or to your relationship with your coach were you to bring these up? What might you gain/learn if you did? What might you need in order to risk bringing them up?

Think about what you want to learn from this session of coaching and how you might present your material.

Immediate preparation for the coaching session:

1. Are there any crises/emergency issues you need to talk about?
2. Are there any themes emerging for you in your overall work you would like to review in coaching?
3. Are there any general organizational/training areas that you want to talk about?
4. What do you want from this session of coaching? For yourself, your team, your organization, your learning?
5. Are there any areas of the coaching contract you want to review/re-negotiate?

(Adapted from: Inskipp and Proctor, 2001).

Appendix 17 has a list of questions that will be helpful to you in preparing for your executive coaching session.

We cannot stress enough the importance of agreeing a clear, achievable, realistic goal/contract with your coach to avoid disappointment and even end up wasting time.

...we will look in some detail at the roles and responsibilities you have as a coachee...

One of the areas you will notice as a prominent heading in the Coaching Contract is "Roles and Responsibilities". Here we will look in some detail at the roles and responsibilities you have as a coachee.

These responsibilities will include:

1. Your learning (objectives).
2. Applying learning from coaching.
3. Keeping notes of coaching sessions.
4. Feedback to self and to coach.
5. Preparing for coaching.

6. Presenting in coaching.

Learning objectives

We suggest that you spend time thinking through your learning objectives from coaching. While, overall, you take responsibility for yourself as a learning adult, here you can specify what objectives you would like to concentrate on within this coaching experience.

Examples of learning objectives are:

1. "To learn how to challenge colleagues more effectively".
2. "To fine-tune my ability to make better focused, clear and energetic presentations".
3. "To work more effectively within this organization".
4. "To facilitate this team in becoming more cohesive in its relationships and its objectives".
5. "To reassess my strengths and assess whether I am working to the best of my ability in line with business goals".
6. "To learn to express my anger in an acceptable manner, rather than 'blasting off' at people".

...Articulating clear learning objectives for yourself in consultation with your coach allows you to have clear end-goals towards which you are working...

Articulating clear learning objectives for yourself in consultation with your coach allows you to have clear end-goals towards which you are working. Agreeing them with your coach allows your coach to monitor these learning objectives for you, and give ongoing feedback on how well you are doing. In this process of setting learning objectives, it is vital to do this in relation to the company agenda if, as is customary, they are the third party in the contract. Where these two agendas are at odds with one another, this will need to be discussed and clarified before proceeding. You may find that what is more suitable for your needs is private counselling, consultation, couple's work, or psychotherapy.

Example

What is your response to the following example?

Peter says in his team coaching group that he wants to discuss his working relationship with a colleague in another department that is in difficulties. When the coach asks how he would describe the difficulty, Peter replies in general terms and with some irritation in his voice: he says he wants to 'get on with it and this is not helpful'. He tells his story and the coach and group members get involved in a long and detailed discussion with Peter of the events of the past few weeks that have generated the 'difficulty'. After half an hour, the coach draws the discussion to a close since others want time to present. At this point Peter says: 'I feel even more confused now than I did when I arrived. I still do not know how to approach my work colleague when I see her again'. Everyone in the group feels disappointed.

Review And Discussion

1. Have you a clear method for preparing for coaching?
2. What are the factors in your life that interfere, just now, with your preparation time? Can you sort them out so that you ensure there is quality time for coaching preparation?
3. How can you ensure that you make clear contracts for your executive coaching?

As a coachee, you will create the coaching agenda. Bring your concerns, joys, worries, problems and celebrations to the coaching sessions. In preparation, you will organize and prioritize what you want from coaching. In presenting your material in coaching, you will want to use the time economically and beneficially.

Presenting In Executive Coaching

A good place to start thinking about the presentation of an issue in coaching is by answering these questions:

1. Why are you bringing this to your coaching session?
2. What are you hoping for from your coach/the coaching in respect to this area?

You can present your material for coaching:

1. Verbally: You tell your story in the coaching session. You can 'tell the story' of a particular problem or interaction or describe an event that you wish to review with your coach in order to find a way forward. In this case you may rely on some notes or on your memory. This can be useful when an overview of a situation is necessary to put a problem or your question in context.
2. Notes: You give your notes in advance to your coach. You can prepare notes of a problem, a conflict, or an area for discussion and e-mail these to your coach in advance so that he/she can read them before the session. This may be useful when you am preparing a presentation or preparing for a review.
3. Process reports: You can also write up a more detailed process report after a meeting and take this to coaching. The advantage is that the coach will get a sense of the ongoing process that you went through as well as the moment-by-moment interactions in the context of the whole event.

...process recording is a way of recording in detail, either during a meeting or an interview or immediately afterwards, what was said by both parties...

Knapman and Morrison (1998) point out that process recording is a way of recording in detail, either during a meeting or an interview or immediately afterwards, what was said by both parties, recording the non-verbal cues given by both parties and any analysis of what you, the coachee, thought might be happening.

Useful triggers can be sections entitled:

1. What I said.
2. What he/she said.
3. What I felt.
4. What I told myself.
5. What I did.
6. What he/she/they did.
7. What seemed to be happening at this point?

Example

Raj arrived for his coaching session with detailed notes he had written up after leading a team meeting. He had sent the coach a copy ahead of the session, so they were both in a position to review the process of the meeting. Although Raj said that the team members had ostensibly reached agreement about objectives under his leadership, he was left feeling uncertain about the process in his team. When Raj and the coach carefully reviewed the interactions described in his notes, it became clear that Raj frequently cut short discussions in order quickly to agree a decision. Several team members were reacting to this by being passive-aggressive and so undermining the process by joking and using other distractions from the task. The executive coaching session enabled Raj to review his leadership style and develop a more collaborative way of managing his team with better results.

Review And Discussion

1. What is the best way for you to present effectively for coaching?
2. What are the pros and cons of different methods of presentation in coaching?
3. How can you connect learning objectives (what you want from executive coaching) to the company agenda.

Keeping Notes Of Coaching Sessions

...This will allow you to review what happened during the coaching session...

We recommend that you keep summary notes of your coaching sessions. During the session, it is always helpful to make notes on insights, ideas, action points and any other decisions made. This will allow you to review what happened during the coaching session and give you a summary of what action points you need to apply to your work. Keeping a "Learning Journal" is a good idea. In it you can summarize your overall learning and see your coaching notes as part of such a journal.

As a coachee, it is your responsibility to incorporate the decisions made during coaching into your work. Having action points is often only the beginning of the process of learning. The final point of the learning curve is when you are able to implement those action points into your work. Outlining plans and ideas of how best to apply your learning to your work is a second stage.

Appendix 16 has a format for helping you capture learnings from your executive coaching session. Have a look at it now and see if might help you fill it in after your sessions.

Example

Janice in her coaching session was working on the process of giving feedback. She made an agreement that her 'homework' task would involve putting into practice giving clear critical and supportive feedback to her team members, which has been stipulated as her primary goal for the coaching. When the coach met up with her again in three weeks' time, she sounded surprised that the coach had expected results 'so soon' after their previous session. Janice was clearly avoiding a process she may well have been more afraid of than she first admitted. Indeed, managing her fear proved to be the subject of further coaching and formed part of an elaborated contract between her and her coach.

Evaluating Executive Coaching As A Coachee

It is important that you have methods of evaluating your coaching sessions and overall coaching arrangements so that you can be sure it is meeting your needs and the needs of the organization who will usually pay for executive coaching.

Here are two forms we use in evaluating coaching – have a look and see if you can adapt them to your situation. The idea is to fill them in and begin a conversation with your coach about the content.

An Evaluation Feedback Form For Executive Coachee

Date of coaching: ....

1. Is your coach providing sufficient support to facilitate your learning?

....

2. Have you identified sufficient and varied opportunities for your learning?

....

3. Is the coaching relationship productive? Is there anything needing to be discussed?

....

4. Is the feedback from your coach thoughtful, candid and constructive?

....

5. Is there a good balance of support and challenge in your coaching?

....

6. Are there areas you do not talk about in coaching that should be the focus of a conversation?

....

7. Is what you are discussing in coaching making impacts on your performance in life or work?

....

8. What seems to you to be the next challenge in your development?

....

9. What is most helpful about your coaching arrangement? What is least helpful?

....

10. Is there anything you would like your coach to stop doing? Start doing? Increase? Decrease?

....

The second form is more focused on an individual coaching session rather than the overall coaching arrangement.

Coaching Session Evaluation

Date of coaching: ....

1. What went particularly well in our coaching session?

....

2. What relationship challenges did we face?

....

3. Were we communicating effectively with each other?

....

4. Were we candid and open in our communication?

....

5. What did we not talk about (avoided)?

....

6. What learning challenges emerged?

....

7. Any external factors that impacted on our coaching session?

....

8. What three strategies could improve the quality of our coaching arrangement?

....

....

....

Example

Juliet rarely prepares for her executive coaching session. She always arrives flustered and stressed (and often late) apologising as she takes off her coat for her poor time keeping, her lack of time to prepare and her general chaotic behaviour. Juliet is all over the place and the session reflects this. Her conversation grass-hops – she moves from one theme to the next without connection or obvious focus which Margaret, her executive coach, tries to make sense of through reflecting back and summarising. It doesn't seem to work much. Margaret is wondering how she might help Juliet structure her use of the executive coaching time better.

Review And Discussion

1. Do you have a clear and helpful method for preparing for your executive coaching sessions?
2. What do you think are the characteristics of dialogue suitable for executive coaching?
3. What kinds of conversation would you like to have with your executive coach?
4. What do you not talk about in your executive coaching sessions that would be helpful for you to focus on?
5. Does your executive coach help you evaluate the coaching sessions and ask you for feedback on them?

Chapter 5:

Issues In Executive Coaching

Understanding Developmental Stages Of Learning As A Coachee

Identifying your own learning style will be an advantage in terms of knowing what helps you most effectively in your coaching sessions. However, before we do this, it may be helpful to reflect on the overall process of learning over time that occurs through the effective use of good coaching. We will outline these stages briefly here.

Stage 1: Relying On Your Own Inner Critic To Coach You

In our experience as executive coaches, we have noticed a tendency for coachee's to come to their first coaching session using their own internal critics as 'coaches'. They often judge themselves and their work very harshly and in a global manner. For example, coachees may say of themselves: "You see: I never get anything right" or "There I go again, stupid as always" or "I constantly make a mess of things" or "I am no good at conflict resolution". Such global statements can be damning of you and your work and do not leave you any room for improvement. In fact, they can often leave you feeling hopeless and devastated. Statements like these often form part of an internal dialogue ie., internal criticisms based on our earlier experiences with significant people who are now 'in our own heads' or simply opinions of ourselves that have never been checked out in a supportive environment where we can receive realistic feedback.

...we may quite understandably have grown reluctant to reveal our lack of knowledge or our need for help in any particular area of work...

Because we may have been shamed or humiliated for 'not knowing' when we were younger, we may quite understandably have grown reluctant to reveal our lack of knowledge or our need for help in any particular area of work. Good coaching provides an opportunity to undo this harmful reticence and provides us with a place where we can truly learn what we want to know! So it may be a good start to identify the unhelpful messages from your own "internal critic" and challenge these for yourself and/or discuss them with your coach and even with your peers.

This first stage thus marks a move from "unconscious incompetence to conscious incompetence" (Robinson, 1974): you get to realize what you do and do not know in your particular area of work. This can at best, result in a realistic setting of learning goals as you identify the areas you need to learn and refine. Sometimes this process of becoming aware of what you still have to learn may leave you feeling deskilled, so it is important to remind yourself that this is a natural part of learning anything new.

Stage 2: The Stage Of The 'Internalized' Coach

We are indebted to Casement (1985) for the concept of the 'internalized' monitor as a stage of development as a learner. In the process of interacting with a coach you will gradually move from drawing on your own inner critic to drawing on the wisdom and experience of your coach. In this process you will "introject" or take into your own internal mental world your real life coach's attitudes and ideas. In practical terms this means using the wisdom and suggestions of your coach to support your work. Following very literally the advice of a coach and even using his/her very words in your dealings with people often mark this stage. This may seem to some of you to represent an over-reliance on your coach, but we see this as a natural stage of the learning process as you gradually allow someone else's ideas to impact on you and to assist you in your work. Coachees at this stage may say to the coach: 'I could hear your voice in my head' or 'I remembered your words as I sat opposite the person I discussed in coaching last time we met'. This marks the process of 'internalizing' the coach and gradually replacing the critic in your head who may have been undermining you rather than helping you to learn, with an image of your own coach. Of course, some of us may resist accepting help from anyone and may reject whatever the coach has to offer. We may rebel at the thought that anyone may know better and feel that accepting help in this way is an admission of defeat and even inadequacy. We may view any acknowledgement of needing advice and help as a sign of 'weakness' and regard our own vulnerability as a fault line in our character that is exacerbated by accepting help from the coach. This attitude will be worth exploring: 'When and where did we decide that accepting help shows weakness?' And is this an attitude that supports our learning and development in the workplace?

At this stage it is important to feel that your coach acknowledges your experience and supports your ongoing development and evolving personal style of being a leader. Both the acknowledgement of your own competencies by yourself and by the coach and the agreeing of appropriate learning goals are important for successful coaching.

This stage marks the movement from 'conscious incompetence to conscious competence' (Robinson, 1974) as you gradually internalize new knowledge and new skills (page 58 names the four stages of this process if you need a reminder). These may still seem a little foreign to you as you may be taking these on in an undigested way from your coach or from other sources of learning. However, you need to take in new ideas and skills before you can fully digest these and make them your own. For each of us, imitation can be a very effective means of learning something new and difficult.

Stage 3: Developing Your Own 'Internal Coach'

...a person is in the process of developing or refining his/her own personal style of learning...

At this stage as a coachee, you begin to develop your own 'internal' coach that integrates what has been learnt from your coach and everything from your own reflections, experimenting, observations, learning and discussions. It is a process of developing your own criteria for effective outcomes in the workplace and being able to judge for yourself when you are being effective or ineffective in your work. At this stage a person is in the process of developing or refining his/her own personal style of learning and of being effective which may, in some ways, be influenced by the coach's style but will have your own unique personal stamp. At this stage you will digest what you have learned and you will change or retain individual elements that suit your style as a person and as a leader.

What we consider important at this stage is that as a coachee you can own your own competence and assess the quality of your work by realistic standards. One of the important processes in developing effective work habits is relinquishing the idea that there is only one right way of doing things and, instead, looking to being as effective as possible in a certain context. This stage marks the move from "conscious competence to unconscious competence" (Robinson, 1974) as we gradually fully integrate what we know and begin to practice our skills and our competence in the workplace without constant vigilance and hesitation. The danger at this point is that you may become a bit too relaxed; so ongoing reflection remains for us an important part of staying in touch with yourself and your work. In the course of daily pressures, setting time aside for review and reflection may seem like a luxury, but having some 'checking in' sessions with your coach at regular intervals several months apart may well support your ongoing development.

Questions To Assess Whether I Am Moving From One Stage To Another

From Stage 1 to Stage 2

1. Am I beginning to challenge myself when I get frustrated because I feel that I am 'not doing things right', and focusing instead on whether my actions are getting the desired result or not?
2. Is the critical 'noise' in my head lessening and being replaced by a more supportive voice that allows me to make mistakes and rectify these?
3. Am I asking for what I really want in coaching or am I still avoiding bringing my mistakes and difficulties?
4. Do I now have a clear idea of my goals so that these are in line with my stage of development in the workplace and clearly known by me and the coach?
5. Am I making effective contracts with my coach so that I am getting all of my learning needs met in coaching?

From Stage 2 to Stage 3

1. Am I beginning to feel more confident about my own decisions when in the workplace?
2. Am I setting realistic and achievable goals in my work and enjoying the satisfaction of reaching these?
3. Do I feel empowered in coaching and in the workplace to explore my own thinking and feelings about situations?
4. Do I allow my coach to 'give' to me and share his/her wisdom or am I not really open to this process?
5. Am I gradually developing my own internal criteria for effectiveness so that I am no longer so dependent on external criticisms or judgements that they render me ineffective?

...gradually developing my own internal criteria for effectiveness so that I am no longer so dependent on external criticisms...

Stage 3 Onwards

1. Do I have clear criteria by which to assess my own work effectiveness?
2. Am I able to judge when I do something well? When I make a mistake, can I remedy it without plunging into shame?
3. Do I generally trust my own judgement, thinking and capacity to make effective choices in my work setting?
4. Do I know when I need help or support? Can I ask for this openly and honestly and from the appropriate people?
5. Am I taking steps to maintain a lively interest in my work by exploring new facets and ideas that engage my interest?

The "Voices Of Different Stages"

The theme and metaphor/symbol of "voice" has been used by a number of authors to depict the element in developmental power that comes our way through life and through relationships. Whyte (1994) captures the idea well: "The voice emerges literally from the body as a representation of our inner world. It carries our experience from the past, our hopes and fear for the future and the emotional resonance of the moment ... the voice is as important to our identity as anything we possess" (pp103-4). Belenky et al (1986) used the image of voice in their groundbreaking research on Woman's Ways of Knowing and we can adapt their notion to looking at the stages that executive coaching sometimes goes through:

1. Silenced. In this first stage coachees are disempowered, unable to hold their own identity and centre and are effectively both passive and ineffective. While they speak they are silenced in the sense that they have no power to influence self or others.
2. Received voice is the stage of those who speak with the voices and tongues of others. You will recognize them as they begin their sentences with: "My boss says...my religion tells me....my parents taught me". They have not yet discovered their own voice so they live by and regurgitate the voices of others more powerful than themselves.
3. Subjective voice is the moment when an individual speaks his or her own words and thoughts. They have spoken for themselves. At this stage the sound of their own voice is sweet music in their own ears and they often shout and rejoice in its sound. They often fail to hear the voices of others at this stage in their development.
4. Critical voice captures the ability of those with their own voice to hear other voices but critically and often as opposed to their own.
5. Constructed voice (which in Chapter 11 we will call dialogue) is the ability to hold my own voice, hear the voices of others, begin conversations that respect both and work together in dialogue towards conclusions that may change and help us both (generative dialogue).

Exercise

Review the five kinds of voice and see if you can tell (from listening to yourself and a few others) from where they speak. What kind of voice best exemplifies your executive coaching arrangement?

Transference And Countertransference In The Coaching Relationship

...It is as though we will be experiencing one another through the lens of the past...

Transference is usually understood to refer to attitudes, feelings and unresolved issues that we bring from the past into our current relationships that influence good relationships in the present. Countertransference would then refer to similar attitudes and feelings on the part of the coach that interfere with his/her capacity to really see and meet the coachee. If we are both carrying 'baggage' from the past into the present, especially if we are not aware of it, then we are unlikely to have a real meeting in the present. It is as though we will be experiencing one another through the lens of the past.

Transference is a possible occurrence in coaching, but may also occur with your boss or others in the workplace who have authority over your work. With some reflection it can usually be readily identified. Often this transference is related to other authority figures from our past with whom we have had conflicts; these unresolved feelings are then projected onto the coach (or the person who referred us for coaching) and we may have difficulty separating out what belongs to the present and what to the past. This can lead to feelings of anger or resentment that may or may not have any basis in the present, but will be seen by others as an overreaction to an event. Not all anger is transference! The distinction is about whether it seems appropriate to the present event or not. However, it may also happen that the coach reminds us of someone we revered in the past, and then this idealization is projected onto the present coach. This may place a heavy burden on the coach to be like someone he/she has never met rather than being himself/herself in the relationship! Such feelings of idealization can help the working alliance to develop but you can see that a more realistic picture of the actual person will gradually need to emerge for you if the relationship is to survive and not end in disappointment. For the coach too, countertransference may be a help or a hindrance in developing a good working alliance. If you have a sense that the coach is not really 'seeing you', then it would be a good idea to raise that matter and discuss your relationship openly so that it is based more realistically in the present.

Questions To Ask Yourself About Transference In The Coaching Relationship.

In the presence of my coach, my boss, others in authority…

1. Do I feel 'small' and 'vulnerable'?
2. Do I have feelings that I have had to other authority figures in my life, parents or teachers?
3. Do I feel very much in awe of my coach?
4. Am I prone to feelings of shame in the coaching session?
5. Am I scared to ask for what I really need?
6. Do I feel as though I have a 'crush' on him/her (the coach)?
7. Do I silence myself in the coaching sessions?

Identifying the transferential feelings will help you to recognize and manage them better as they arise. You may even make this recognition a part of the coaching contract with an agreement that you will not allow these feelings to disempower you and prevent you from getting your learning needs met. Clear open communication about needs and feelings is the best way through to a more effective working alliance.

(**Note:** If you are interested in reading further about transference in the workplace, we refer you to the book entitled "The Leader on the Couch" by Manfred Kets de Vries, 2007 especially chapters 2 and 9).

Dealing With My 'Drivers' In Executive Coaching

…Essentially a driver is our translation of a message meant to help us work more effectively…

The concept of 'drivers' derives from Transactional Analysis (Kahler 1974;1978) and refers to ways in which we take on common 'parental' messages from our culture and then use these to push and drive and berate ourselves. Essentially a driver is our translation of a message meant to help us work more effectively and turning this into a stick with which to beat ourselves! We speak of 'driver' behaviour as having a driven quality to it because it is lacking in spontaneity and creativity. It is essentially compulsive behaviour which does not allow for reflection and imagination, but drives us ever onward to do things rather than to pause to 'be' fully in the present. We will review here the common 'drivers' in our culture and you can check as you read these whether any of them hold any power for you.

The 'Be Perfect' Driver

People with this 'driver' are constantly pushing themselves to do things 'perfectly' without any mistakes. They can often get stuck because they are trying to get a particular detail (for example, the opening sentence to a document) 'just right' and so may never get to finish a job. They may have been told 'If a job is worth doing, it is worth doing it well' which is eminently good advice but has become translated into needing everything to be 'perfect' - an impossible goal in an imperfect world! All drivers contain an element of good advice, in this case that an attention to detail is important in many jobs. However, it is the compulsive attempt to perfect everything before moving on that constitutes this 'driver' behaviour. In this person's world there are to be no mistakes; and the idea that we may learn from our mistakes and experiments is anathema to them. They want to get it right the first time as if there is never going to be another chance to correct their mistakes. In fact, they believe that you only have one chance at things and if you miss that, that is the end! They also use the words 'right' and 'wrong' frequently as though there is a perfectly 'right' way of doing everything. You can already hear what pressure this may place on a person and how little room it leaves for learning from our mistakes. You may become so focused on 'getting it right' that you may not get any of your own actual learning needs met in coaching.

The 'Please Others' Driver

...it is important in any work context that we can co-operate with others and consider their needs and demands...

This 'driver' involves the person in over-adapting to the needs and demands of others whilst sacrificing his/her own. This person is compulsively pleasing and struggles when anyone is displeased with him/her or any aspect of his/her behaviour. They want to be 'liked' at all costs, even if this requires foregoing their own needs and demands in a situation. Of course, it is important in any work context that we can co-operate with others and consider their needs and demands in an adult and considerate manner. Team work is essential to good functioning at work, and to be a good team member does require some accommodation of others. But it is the driven nature of the 'please others' driver that leaves this person little space or time to consider his/her own needs and opinions in any situation. They struggle with displeasing others and will avoid conflict at all costs even if they suffer as a result.

A person with a 'please others' driver will have over-adapted to parental figures in childhood and these patterns can be very persistent. In coaching, this person may try to second guess what the coach 'wants' and will work out how to please the coach rather than focusing on his/her own needs in the workplace.

The 'Try Hard' Driver

People with this driver often believe that everything in life is difficult and that they will struggle with whatever they undertake. They may have a frown on their faces regularly and talk about their struggles, seldom focusing on achievements or completed tasks. As children, these people have often received the message that they will struggle but not achieve success so that they are left believing that there is virtue in trying hard even if they never succeed at anything. They will not allow themselves space to play and be creative and imaginative, as though those processes are forbidden. They may also focus unhelpfully on mistakes and not accept them as an opportunity for learning, but regard them instead as irreparable fault-lines in their characters and inevitable for people like themselves. They will bring this struggle to coaching and to the workplace and find it hard to learn anything new without regarding their lack of knowledge as some basic character flaw in themselves. Their biggest challenge is to begin to experience learning as fun and to realize and enjoy successes.

The 'Be Strong' Driver

...some degree of independence and self-reliance is important in a work context...

This person believes in keeping a 'stiff upper lip' and not admitting to any vulnerability or need for dependence on others. The central belief is that it is important to be strong at all times in all situations; to 'cope on my own' rather than needing anything from others or in any way depending on them for assistance. Of course some degree of independence and self-reliance is important in a work context, but to persist in compulsively being strong when you need help, and could readily receive this from others, is the hallmark of this 'be strong driver' behaviour. Again, it is the compulsive nature of the behaviour that interferes with effective functioning. This person will have particular difficulty in bringing any vulnerabilities, mistakes or needs to coaching, believing that the coach will see this as a source of weakness and incompetence. Permission to get it wrong and bring mistakes to coaching is crucial to the person with the 'be strong' driver.

The 'Hurry Up' Driver

The person with this driver behaviour is always in a hurry and will never pause or take things slowly. Time for reflection, for play and for creative thinking is often regarded as a waste of time. Of course, there are times when doing a job speedily and efficiently are really vital to the success of a task. However, the person with the 'hurry up' driver will be rushing all the time often at the cost of doing things carefully and allowing time for revision or checking for mistakes. This person was often not allowed to move at his/her own pace as a child and so learnt to rush at everything in order to avoid chastisement. This driven compulsive pattern can become really counterproductive in situations where a more measured and careful approach will get better results. The person with this driver often comes to coaching with a list that he/she hurries through, not leaving much time for discussion, reflection or imaginative thinking. This makes learning a chore to be completed rather than an enjoyable and creative process. He/she will struggle if slowed down to reflect and generate different options and ideas, although this is really the permission he most needs from the coach, for example, permission to carry some less urgent issues over to the next session!

Most of us do not just possess one driver but may manifest a combination of these in a hierarchy of importance. For example, we may please others by being perfect or try hard to be strong! You have probably realized by now that these compulsive driver behaviours are the opposite of creative, spontaneous playful learning, working and living. They all add an element of pressure into work and into coaching that interferes fundamentally with our competence, enjoyment, effectiveness and spontaneity.

Go to Appendix 14 if you would like to fill in the Drivers Checklist and rate yourself on the above.

Getting It Wrong

We are devoting a separate section to the idea of 'getting it wrong' because we so often meet people in all contexts who believe that there is only one 'right' way to do something and that if they do not find it, they are somehow inferior or inadequate! We substitute the idea of "effective outcomes" for 'getting it right' so that people start evaluating what they do in terms of the goals that they set themselves, rather than feeling caught in a right/wrong dynamic. Many people who come to us for coaching have had the experience of an educational system in which they were severely shamed for making mistakes or getting it wrong in the eyes of authority. This may have been combined with little understanding of their particular struggles or little attempt to help them remedy or learn from mistakes. In many ways this shame-based educational process feeds into the driver behaviour outlined above and mitigates against any true learning or creativity and spontaneity of expression. One of our first principles is that there are no absolute 'right' ways of doing jobs, of learning or of communicating, but only more or less effective ways depending on the outcome you desire and the field conditions at any moment. Often the idea of doing it right has got caught up in morality as though it is immoral to make a mistake! We stress that making a mistake is part of the learning process throughout life. And that striving to behave within your own moral code and with integrity may nevertheless mean making mistakes and learning from these!

Exercise

How might you manage the following situation?

Imagine that you are a coachee and you are meeting a new coach. As you deal with the introductions, you begin to get a similar feeling to one you had in primary school with one of your teachers who would often punish children by getting them to stand alone in front of the class holding their 'failed' work. How would you deal with this situation?

...if the feeling persists, you may want to check if there are any similarities in the here-and-now situation to the past...

You may start by having an internal dialogue with yourself about how this is not your teacher but the coach and this is 20 years later and this coaching contract is your choice. However, if the feeling persists, you may want to check if there are any similarities in the here-and-now situation to the past, and consider addressing with the coach what you may want of him/her that will meet your needs in the present situation. Often in situations like this, people either 'get stuck' in an unproductive relationship or leave the situation. Addressing clearly what your needs are and contracting for these may well deal with the difficulty.

Review And Discussion

1. Have you a sense of the stages that coachees go through on their journey to becoming more confident in the coaching relationship and in the workplace?
2. Where are you on this journey and what are the tasks and challenges that you face just now?
3. What are the skills you bring to your work just now?
4. Can you see how transference might work within coaching, the workplace and more generally in life situations?
5. Have you worked out for yourself what are your "drivers"?

Chapter 6

Skills For Executive Coachees

Introduction

The following six chapters will present six key skills on which being an effective executive coachee are based. In our experience, the more you are able to practice these skills, the more you will be able to use executive coaching as a highly effective learning relationship. The six skills are:

1. Learning how to learn.
2. Learning how to give and receive feedback.
3. Learning realistic self-evaluation.
4. Learning how to reflect.
5. Learning emotional awareness.
6. Learning how to dialogue.

We will look in some detail at each of these key skills in turn.

Coachee Skill 1: Learning How To Learn

...This section is to help you, the coachee understand what learning is and what your particular style of learning is...

Throughout this booklet we have insisted that executive coaching is a relationship whose purpose is to encourage and support the learning of coachees. Executive coaching is personalized or customized learning. Effective coaches tailor-make their strategies and interventions to match the learning style of coachees. This section is to help you, the coachee understand what learning is and what your particular style of learning is. Individuals have their preferred ways of learning and learn at different paces. We also know that learning is influenced by social interaction, interpersonal relationship and communications with others, by past experiences of learning and past learning relationships. How power is exercised in relationships has a surprisingly powerful influence on learning. Researchers have framed how an imbalance of power in a relationship can affect learning outcomes, especially for those who are already experiencing some kind of marginalization. Women and individuals from ethnic minorities can experience relationships where they do not feel understood or listened to – the power differential can be used to disempower them or make them feel invisible.

Some people learn primarily by doing, others by reflecting, others by theorising and again, others love to learn by applying theory to practice (see Appendix 8 for Honey and Mumford's Learning Styles Inventory).

Our question for you is:

How do you learn?

We are making a distinction between teaching and learning. In teaching, the teacher asks you to join him/her in their world. In learning, the teacher joins you in your world. For us, effective coaches are flexible and move towards their coachees. They see it as their task to find out how coachees learn and then adapt their teaching strategies to facilitate learning. But executive coaches can only do that when they know what the individualized learning format of their coachee is. Some coaches use a "one size fits all" concept of learning ie., that all coachees learn in the same way. We think this is unfortunate and results in forcing some coachees to learn in ways that are not appropriate for them.

Exercise

What has been the most significant learning in your life in the past 5 years? WHY?

Who has been the most significant person in your learning? WHY?

If you could learn something that would make a huge difference in your life just now, what is it? WHY DON'T YOU LEARN IT?

The point of this exercise is to help you begin to think of how you learn, what kinds of people facilitate your learning and what blocks your learning. Look in particular at your answers to the questions WHY and WHY DON'T YOU LEARN? Make a list that will include:

1. *What helps you learn best? Where, What, Who, How?*
2. *What blocks your learning?*
3. *Where have you been blocked in the past?*
4. *What helped you unblock your learning?*
5. *Who are the best people to help you learn?*

Exercise

What is learning? Have a look at some definitions and make some notes of what they mean to you in the light of the exercise above.

"Learning is what you do when you don't know what to do" (Claxton, 1999).

"Learning is the changes a person makes in himself or herself that increase the know-why and/or the know-what and/or the know-how the person possesses in respect of a given subject" (Vaill, 1996:21).

"Learning is the process of using a prior interpretation to construe a new or revised interpretation of the meaning of one's experience as a guide to future action" (Mezirow, 2000:7).

"Learning is a persisting change in performance or performance potential that results from experience and interaction with the world" (Driscoll, 2005).

...Coaching, like other relational approaches to learning, will be helped or hindered by the cultural environment of your organization...

Later on we will look at different levels of learning and types of learning (eg., knowledge, skills, capabilities, attitudes etc). For now, we want to see if we can understand learning in general. Learning is not an isolated event that takes place away from the workplace or the organization of which you are a part. Mezirow (2000) who coined the term transformational learning argues that "the who, what, when, where, why and how of learning may be only understood as situated in a specific cultural context" (p.7). Coaching, like other relational approaches to learning, will be helped or hindered by the cultural environment of your organization and the messages it gives about learning. You might want to stop here for a moment to think about what learning means in your organization.

Some questions:

1. Do you feel that your manager supports and encourages your ongoing learning?
2. Do you think your organization dictates or controls what and how you learn?
3. How open is your organization to new learning? To feedback?

The answers to these questions might give you some insights into what learning means for you in your specific environment.

Adult Learning

...you will be asked to take responsibility for implementing some of these principles...

You are an adult learning and therefore the principles of adult learning will apply to you. As an adult learner, you will be asked to take responsibility for implementing some of these principles and for working with your executive coach to create the optimum learning environment and relationship. We called this manual "creating learning partnerships" because we believe like Martin Buber that "all learning takes place in relationship" and that the right kind of relationship makes all the difference where learning is at stake.

Some of the principles of adult learning are:

1. Adults learn best when they take responsibility for their own learning ie., they are internally motivated to learn.
2. Adult learning depends on adults being involved in planning, implementing and evaluating their own learning.
3. Self-direction is important for adult learning.
4. Adults learn best when they are in touch with their own particular way of learning (auditory, visual, kinesthetic).
5. For adults, emotions are as much a part of learning as is intellect.
6. Adults respond, like all learners, to a facilitative learning environment and good learning relationships.
7. Adults respond particularly well to experiential learning.
8. Language is a key part of learning.

You can probably add other factors to these principles that affect and help your learning (challenge, feedback, support, groups you belong to, reading, etc). Have another look at these principles and see how many of them are in place in your executive coaching arrangement.

Peter Hawkins and Nick Smith (2006) have put together what they have called the "Golden Threads" that people like executive coaches need to be aware of to ensure the environment is conducive to learning.

Golden Threads:

1. There is always more than one client you serve. This is true even when you are coaching or mentoring an individual executive.
2. All real time learning and development is relational.
3. Robust dialogue that balances challenge and support is essential for relationships to develop and individuals to learn.
4. Learning is for life, not just for courses.
5. Adult human beings learn best through experience not by being taught or told. The work of the learning enabler is never to know better and never to know first, but to create the enabling conditions and experiences that create a transformational shift in the relationship and the individual.
6. Transformational change becomes systemic when we focus on the shift in the part of the system we are working directly with (individual, team functions etc.) to jointly create the shift that is necessary in the wider system.

7. Supervision is essential for the coach, mentor or consultant to remain effective and continue to develop (2006: 4 -5).

They also include a section on core principles of learning which again, is worth applying to your coaching situation:

1. Start and end with a focus on self-awareness, developed through experiential learning processes.
2. Use theory only when experiential learning has already got underway.
3. Use "just-in-time learning". Learning is most effective when the learner has already recognized the need for that piece of learning and can apply the learning close to receiving it.
4. Develop authority, presence and impact.
5. Use feedback, coaching, mentoring or change work with peers.
6. Teach basic skills and techniques in a way that bring things alive in the room, using demonstrations, stories, engagement and trainees reflecting on their lived experiences. Employ opportunities for practice and feedback.
7. Real time learning: address real issues that are current and unresolved, rather than case studies from the past. Use real play rather than role play.
8. Supervised practice allows integration between self awareness, skills, theory and the experience of practice.
9. Transformational learning requires unlearning as much as learning. We need to confound our current patterns of behaviour and ways of seeing the world, as well as comprehending new ways of being.
10. Allow the learner to exceed the teacher's capacity (Hawkins and Smith, 2006: 112).

There are many ways of thinking about learning:

1. Knowledge, information, models, theories and frameworks. This is usually intellectual knowledge eg., reading up on team development.
2. Skills that allow us to do more, relate better, solve problems or work in teams (by skills we mean the abilities to do something well).
3. Accessing intelligences rather than overusing our preferred intelligence (Gardner, 1999; Goleman, 1996, 1998; Zohar and Marshall, 2000) increases our learning and our learning about learning.
4. Knowing our learning style and the learning styles of others can assist as we set up learning experiences for ourselves and others (Honey and Mumford, 1995).
5. Transformational learning investigates the assumptions and beliefs we bring to our learning. In looking at the underlying structure of our ways of knowing (of how we make sense of our world) we come to know, and begin to question whether these assumptions and beliefs curtail or advance our learning.
6. Experiential learning allows us insight from reflection after action. We act, reflect on our actions, learn from our reflection and apply new learning to our tasks.
7. Internal learning pulls us within to look at our values, our way of being, and our self-awareness. In going within, we learn how to manage ourselves, how to build personal qualities for our lives, how to liberate potential and in particular, learn how to learn.
8. Tacit learning is that store of learning we have without sometimes realizing we have it – ways of doing things without knowing how or why.
9. Intuition – a non-rational way of knowing which allows us to come to decisions and find ways of doing things without going though the rational process.

From the above we are suggesting three levels of learning:

1. The WHAT of learning: information, theories, frameworks, and skills
2. The HOW of learning: understanding how you learn in your own particular way
3. The WHY of learning: discovering why you learn the way you do.

Figure 6.1 outlines various aspects of these ways of learning:

Level	Strength	Limitation	Methods	Result
1	Problem solving Information Skills	Nothing changes Head knowledge Incongruence Never question	Lecturing Reading Theories Frameworks Skills training	Knowledge Skills
2	Know my style I own my learning Use variety	Individualistic Reject knowledge Only one voice	Experiential learning Lifelong learning Feedback Reflection	Personal insight Emotions
3	Ongoing change Process	Individualistic No real world Subjectivity	Dialogue Questioning Reflection Dilemmas	Transforming Questioning

Figure 6.1: Levels of Learning

Exercise

Using Table 6.1, begin to think of what level of learning comes easily to you and which levels are difficult.

Different Forms Of Intelligences

...there are different types of intelligences – not just one, intellectual...

Gardner (1999) has suggested that there are different types of intelligences – not just one, intellectual. We have added another one: spiritual intelligence, from Zohar and Marshall (2000). Have a look at these and see which intelligence best defines you or which you best prefer using.

Gardner's Seven Intelligences

1. Linguistic: Language, writing, story telling, and poetry. Sensitivity to words and their sounds: puns and poems. Learn through listening, writing, reading and discussing. Predominately auditory system.
2. Mathematical and Logical: problem solvers who delight in sequence, order and logic. Deductive and inductive reasoning. They are good at solving puzzles and abstract thinking, see the pattern in things. They are good also at hard data, evidence, assessments and hypotheses. Seek harmony and order.
3. Visual and Spatial: Being able to see things from different angles. Able to visualize and imagine scenes. Uses imagination and learns through models and diagrams.
4. Musical: Discern patterns in sound and enjoy experimenting with them, show sensitivity to mood changes and pick out individual sounds, aware of changes within themselves from music, good sense of rhythm. Will enjoy singing.

5. Interpersonal: learns by entering the world of others and makes sense of it. Learns from group experiences and collaborative learning. Good at social relationships and learns from them, good influencers and listeners.
6. Intrapersonal: knowledge about self – can access one's own moods and feelings. Learns from inner world and seeks explanations from within. Values personal growth, enjoys reflective times.
7. Kinesthetic: uses the body as learning method eg., artists, dancers, actors, machinists, and jewellers. Learns from touch, movement, manipulation and physical experience. Will enjoy action and doing eg., field trips.

and…

8. Spiritual: "The intelligence with which we address and solve problems of meaning and value, the intelligence with which we can place our lives in a wider, meaning-giving context, the intelligence with which we can assess that one course of action or one life-path is more meaningful than another" (Zohar and Marshall, 2000).

Exercise

Appendices 8 and 9 include two outlines to help you focus on your learning style and will help you to discern which intelligence seems to be more suited to you. Stop here and do both.

Exercise

In the light of your knowledge and insights from the previous exercise, imagine that I will be your executive coach. Can you answer some questions for me?

1. How can I best facilitate your learning?
2. What can I do that helps you learn best?
3. What blocks your learning?
4. What might I do that would block your learning? And unblock it?
5. How might differences between us impact on our coaching relationship?

Exercise

Have a look at the teaching strategies in Appendix 12 and see, as you go through them, which ones seem to suit your style of learning best. Can you share these with your executive coach so that he/she has some insights into how best to facilitate your learning?

Conclusion

…good insights into your particular style and method of learning…

Our hope is that, at this stage, you have some good insights into your particular style and method of learning and can begin to negotiate with your coach about how he/she can facilitate that learning.

Example

...Her coach asks her about her learning style and how best he can accommodate her...

Asha is meeting her executive coach for the first time where they are drawing up their two way coaching contract. Her coach asks her about her learning style and how best he can accommodate her learning. Asha is puzzled and realizes she has never been asked that question before, "How do you learn"? If you were Asha's executive coach how might you help her find answers to that question?

Review And Discussion

1. Can you begin to describe what learning styles exist and what different types of learning take place?
2. Could you now outline for me your style of learning?
3. If I was your executive coach, how best could I facilitate your learning in coaching?
4. What are the main challenges for you as a learner?

Chapter 7

Coachee Skill 2: Learning How To Give And Receive Feedback

Exercise

Before considering feedback, you might want to fill in the following:

1. *When someone says to you, "I want to give you some feedback", what do you think? What do you feel? What do you do?*
2. *Does your reaction to giving (or receiving) feedback vary if delivered one-to-one versus feedback in a group?*
3. *Think back to your family of origin. Generally speaking, when you received feedback as a child, what did you feel?*
4. *After you have given someone feedback, have you ever wished that you had been more direct in what you had said?*
5. *Complete this sentence: "I feel more comfortable giving (or receiving) feedback when…"*

Do any of the following statements apply to you in respect of giving feedback?

…I don't want to increase distance between myself and the other person…

1. *I don't want to upset anyone or things. So best keep quiet.*
2. *If I wait long enough the situation will resolve itself.*
3. *It's not important enough to make a fuss over.*
4. *I don't want to increase distance between myself and the other person.*
5. *Criticising others reflects badly on me.*
6. *These are good people – they will know when they are getting things wrong.*
7. *I want others to take responsibility – giving feedback takes that away.*
8. *I've made mistakes too so who am I to tell others what to do?*
9. *I find it very upsetting when I have to deliver strong negative feedback.*
10. *I told him twice and it hasn't made any difference, so why bother?*
11. *I don't know if I have enough evidence to confront him.*
12. *I could be wrong about this – perhaps she is right.*
13. *How can I criticize someone who is a friend – good friends don't do that!*
14. *I feel really bad if I upset someone, and giving feedback upsets others at times.*
15. *I am afraid I might get angry if I really say what I want to say.*
16. *She has a very bitter tongue and I would come off worse if there were a fight.*
17. *I don't like receiving feedback myself, so why should I impose it?*
18. *It will only embarrass both of us if I bring that up.*
19. *I don't like him anyway – I would be giving feedback for the wrong reasons.*

Introduction

Of all the skills that executive coaches and executive coachees can possess, "giving feedback" is perhaps the most sophisticated and difficult. We know all too well the harm that results from receiving feedback that destroys us (killer feedback, as someone once called it). Killer feedback hurts, wounds, shames and humiliates and does little to contribute to learning. Part of the problem with feedback is that we remember the feedback we received at the hands of others as children and it was frequently anything but positive (not much has changed it seems: children still receive, on average, seven negatives to every one positive). That is why people rarely ask for feedback, even to help their learning. Otherwise we could regularly ask:

1. What is it like living with me?
2. What feedback would you like to give me as your parent, child, and manager?
3. What would you like to tell us about our being your employer?

4. How am I doing as your executive coach?

Dangerous questions, these. But why? You would think that we would ask for continual feedback in order to learn. "Tell me…..so that I can learn". But we are frightened we might hear what we fear most – I am no good, I should not be here, I am not worthwhile. We anticipate that all feedback will be negative and destructive because often that is the way it was in the past.

…feedback that is well given and received is one of the best sources of learning…

On the other hand, feedback connected to learning and feedback that is well given and received is one of the best sources of learning for all of us. Think back to a moment when someone gave you valuable feedback that made a difference in your life. It probably was not easy to hear but when you heard it, it became a significant learning in your life.

We want to learn, with you, how to give and receive feedback that is connected to learning.

Why Feedback?

Feedback is necessary because there is much about ourselves that we do not know. We are often blind to the effects our behaviours have on others. We have blind spots, deaf spots and dumb spots. Scharmer (2007) has a worthwhile grid that can help us name some of these "spots":

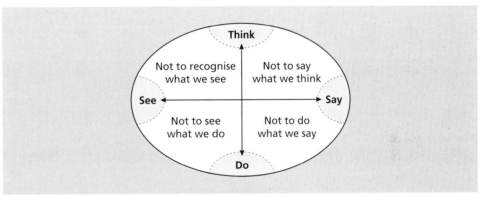

Figure 7.1: Scharmer (2007).

There are things about ourselves we just don't know, either because we do not want to know (we are in denial) or because no one has ever told us and it is outside of our awareness. Knowing how you are perceived and experienced by others has always been important as a learning process. Knowledge about self in relation to others (how I relate to others, work with them, engage with them, talk to them, teach them etc) gives us the insights we need to help us being to change our behaviours. Such knowledge is vital for the effective working of teams and organizations.

It is a well established psychological principle that we judge ourselves by our intentions and we judge others by their behaviour. Our own feedback to ourselves comes from an internal awareness of what our intentions are: on the other hand we go "external" in our evaluations of others' behaviours. We judge what we see. Hence the discrepancy in how we and others see the same behaviour. The racist says: "I am no racist" (and from an intentionality perspective that is true – in their own minds their intention is to "tell the truth as they see it"). I do not see their intentions, I see their behaviour and we define racism by what we do (not by what we intend). I see the discrimination, the prejudice at work and the words that are part of the truth. This is one of the reasons why feedback is so important: it helps all of us who focus on our intentions, to hear another perspective – that of the outsider.

Example

Nigel is unaware that he gets frustrated and angry when his challenges in the team do not work as effectively as he hopes. When he challenges and the recipient does not respond as he had expected, he becomes impatient and ends up bullying. As we watched the video together, I asked him about his intentions regarding Alan, a member of his team. "I want to challenge him to look at his aggressive behaviour, and so I confront him with the inconsistencies between what he says and what he does" replies Nigel. "What happens then?" I probe. "I challenge him clearly and firmly," says Nigel, "but when he ignores me I go after him." I (his executive coach) then give him feedback on what I see, namely that he begins to challenge well but the challenge descends into harassment when he loses his patience and cannot stay with the pace of the this member of his team. Nigel responds with interest, "You're right, I wanted to challenge and ended up harassing; what I need to watch is how impatient I get and how often I do not go at the other person's pace."

Clearly Nigel does not deny what is happening and is using feedback to learn about himself, his style and his way of interaction. Pat, on the other hand, denies what is going on: "How dare you tell me my presentation skills are only average? I have been doing this for four years now and no one has ever said that to me".

What Is Feedback?

...Feedback gives people information that helps them learn and grow...

Feedback is information on behaviour (observable behaviours are the focus) and the effects that that behaviour has on others. Rock (2006) put it well when he describes feedback as "the delicate art of letting people know the score. Feedback gives people information that helps them learn and grow" (p. 203). It can be either confirmatory (want more of it) or corrective (want less of it) or reflective (hold it up to the light to review it). The purpose of feedback is to facilitate learning and help change behaviour. That is why, in giving feedback, people need to be aware of their own motivation for doing it. If you are giving feedback for other reasons than to help the other person learn, then this invalidates the purpose of feedback. Clear, brief sentences based on observable behaviour (without using qualifiers) are best. And its purpose is to help the recipient LEARN, not to put them down, deskill, humble or demotivate them. However, we have already looked at what impacts negatively on our learning. Rock (2006) summarizes these well, "When we experience anxiety, fear, self-consciousness or any strong emotion, our neurons get flooded with electrical signals, so there's not enough capacity left to process what is going on in the moment. We literally stop hearing and seeing what's around us" (p.61). It's worth remembering that if feedback is to be effective (as a learning format) then it has be given within a relationship and an environment that does not cause the above reactions.

Feedback consists of the following:

1. The **what** of feedback (what do I want to say?).
2. The **how** of feedback (how I say it?).

3. The **emotions** of feedback. (emotional barriers are the main obstacles inhibiting the exchange of feedback – how will I deal with emotions, my own and those of others?).
4. The **when** of feedback (the right moment to give feedback).
5. The **where** of feedback (the right place to give feedback).

Exercise

…an example of someone (in the past) that you would have liked to have given feedback to…

Take an example of someone (in the past) that you would have liked to have given feedback to and see if you can use the features above to formulate how you might say it to them.

Exercise

Here is another exercise to help you gain insights into what helps and hinders you from giving and receiving feedback:

Giving Feedback:

Helps

....

Hinders

....

Receiving Feedback:

Helps

....

Hinders

....

Some of the elements you will need to consider when giving and receiving feedback are:

1. Our own background and learning: strong cultural and family background influences encourage us to be nice to people and not say things that make them uncomfortable. "Don't cause conflict" is often a dictate we inherit from the past.
2. We sometimes equate feedback with criticism. There is some evidence that childhood feedback was painful for most people and that there is a connection between past negative experiences of feedback and the ability to receive it in the present. (**Think back to your experience of receiving feedback as a child – what was it like?**)
3. Our difficulty with causing conflict (**is conflict a problem for you?**)
4. How will the other person interpret it: will they feel or be hurt? (**Are you anxious about the person receiving feedback?**)
5. Difficulty of self esteem; we are sometimes worried that if we give negative feedback that we will damage the positive self-image or the self-esteem of the

person to whom we give this feedback. Part of this worry may well be that if the recipient has a negative reaction, we may suffer a collapse in our own self esteem.

6. We know that feedback is often connected not just to our behaviour but to how we see ourselves as persons. At times this connects with our fear that we are no good and not worth loving.

7. We think, at times, that we have no permission to comment on the behaviour and skills of another person.

Giving And Receiving Feedback

...it is worth reminding ourselves of what is helpful or not helpful...

In giving feedback and also in receiving it, it is worth reminding ourselves of what is helpful or not helpful:

	Helpful	Unhelpful
1.	**Helpful**	**Unhelpful**
2.	Behavioural	Attitudinal
3.	Descriptive	Evaluative
4.	Specific	General (vague)
5.	Two-sided	One-sided
6.	Solicited	Unsolicited
7.	Current	Historic
8.	Relevant	Irrelevant
9.	Offered	Imposed
10.	Checked	Unchecked
11.	Recognizes emotion	Ignores emotion
12.	Open	Closed
13.	Ongoing	Occasional
14.	Expected	Unexpected

Exercise

Go back to the exercise above where you were giving feedback to someone from your past and run it through the above characteristics.

A key to effective feedback is to understand the other in terms of:

1. His/her way of learning: emotional, intellectual, etc.
2. How much time do they need to talk through the feedback?
3. Ability to hear undefensively (how defended are they?).
4. How able are they to be in touch with themselves?
5. How am I perceived and experienced by the other person?

Occasionally, when feedback goes wrong, we can trace it to the following:

1. Burying the message so that it is unclear.
2. Playing the psychologist and interpreting the inner meaning of what is going on.
3. Questioning that becomes interrogation.
4. Softening, disclaiming or apologising for the feedback.
5. Agreement that is not real agreement (pretending to agree).
6. Going on and on without stopping to check in or listen back.
7. Not including any positive feedback.

Reactions of the receiver:

1. Playing the wounded animal (hurt, devastated, wounded, exaggerated).
2. Changing the subject.
3. Attacking as the best form of defence.
4. Using comparisons with others (lobbying).
5. Becoming the masochist/martyr and inviting more negative feedback (punish me more!).

Steps to consider before giving Feedback

...Am I open to changing my views in the light of the discussion...

1. How can I create the most conducive environment for the person to receive the feedback I intend on giving?
2. How do I ensure an open rapport and free interchange?
3. Is the person ready to hear what I want to say?
4. What would stop me giving feedback just now?
5. How am I feeling about giving feedback just now?
6. Am I open to changing my views in the light of the discussion?
7. Am I clear about what I want to share?
8. Am I giving this feedback from a place of goodwill, ie., to help learning?
9. Are there differences in power that can make giving this feedback acceptable?
10. What other contextual issues need I consider before giving feedback?

When giving Feedback. How can I...

1. Bring about an open rapport and a free interchange?
2. Know whether the person is ready and in what state of mind?
3. Keep comments close to the events described?
4. Ensure agreement?
5. Keep in touch with what is happening to me?
6. Be open to changing my own opinion?
7. Know when it might be helpful to refrain from giving feedback?
8. Be aware of the emotional barriers that can make giving and receiving feedback very difficult?
9. Make sure that feedback is not just positive and/or negative: it is well-rounded feedback on how someone is doing?
10. Check that what you intended to say was heard?
11. What are the areas that need improvement/change?
12. How will that improvement or change take place?

After Giving Feedback

Spend a little time reviewing the meeting. Is there something to be filed away for the next meeting?

1. What did I learn about myself?
2. What did I learn about the other person?
3. What did I learn about giving feedback?

Exercise:

The following is a short exercise to help you prepare for receiving feedback and to be open to learning during a feedback session.

Preparing myself to listen:

1. *Am I anxious about what another person might say?*
2. *What would stop me from listening?*
3. *Am I feeling defensive? Attacked?*
4. *How do I feel about the person who is giving me feedback?*
5. *Am I open to what others will say?*

Before the feedback session, ask yourself:

1. *Do I want to learn from this session?*
2. *Am I open to what the other person is going to say?*
3. *Do I want to consider how what is said can help me develop either personally and/or professionally?*
4. *Am I in the right frame of mind to engage with this feedback?*
5. *Can I see this feedback as about my behaviour?*

Listen carefully to what is said by the person or persons giving you feedback.

1. *Articulate feelings, especially if you are finding it difficult to hear the feedback being given.*
2. *Summarize what is said so that the content can be agreed.*
3. *Ask for clarification, if needed, or specifics or examples.*
4. *Own the feedback (make it yours) fully or partially. Or disagree with it after considering it. Discuss it.*
5. *Begin to dialogue about how the feedback can be used to help you practice new behaviours.*
6. *Agree what needs to be done, with whose help, by what date.*
7. *End feedback session.*

The Theory Of Core Qualities

The Theory of Core Qualities (Ofman, 2002) is a model devised for HR managers on how to give negative feedback in a positive and constructive manner. Have a look and see if you can use it in your executive coaching relationship to find areas you need to work on for yourself or indeed to give feedback to self and others.

The model suggests four interconnected angles leading to a quadrant. The four are:

...Core qualities are positive and the strength of an individual and present mostly in their lives...

1. Core Qualities are attributes that form part of a person's core. Those who know the individual will recognize the qualities immediately. Core qualities are positive and the strength of an individual and present mostly in their lives. Examples of core qualities are: determination, loyalty, empathetic, hard working, courage, humility, flexibility etc. Core qualities are recognized by what others appreciate in me, what I expect/demand from others and often what I play down in myself.

2. The Pitfall is when an individual exercises too much of their core quality. The philosophy behind this is that our weaknesses are not the opposites of our strengths but too much of our actual strength:

Determination becomes pushiness or control when taken too far

1. Loyalty becomes collusion.
2. Empathy becomes enmeshment.
3. Helpfulness becomes interference.

...recognize areas for your Pitfall by what you are willing to forgive in others...

The Pitfall is an overdeveloped core quality. It is the area where most of us get negative feedback. You can recognize areas for your Pitfall by what you are willing to forgive in others, what others blame you for (negative feedback) and often by what you try to justify in yourself.

3. The Challenge is the direct opposite of the Pitfall and combined with the Core Quality keeps individuals out of the Pitfall. You will know your challenges by: what you miss in yourself, what you admire in others and what others want for you.

1. So determination needs patience so as to not end up as pushiness.
2. Flexibility needs orderliness so as not to become inconsistency.
3. Loyalty needs objectivity or questioning as not to end up as collusion.

4. The Allergy is a reaction to too much of our challenge and the opposite of the Core Quality. It is what I cannot stand in myself and in others. You will know it by: what you despise in others, what I would hate in myself.

Example

Let's run an example through the Theory of Core Qualities. One of us (Michael) is the executive coach to a Project Manager (Jeremy) in a large company. Jeremy phones up unexpectedly to make an appointment, very upset by an event that has happened in his workplace. On arrival he launches into his story about being labelled "a bully" or "someone who harasses". This has upset him greatly as he has never envisaged himself as such. Briefly, the event happened during a meeting with one of his staff, a new graduate who is working with him on a particular project. Three hours into their meeting she suddenly puts her head in her hands and shouts at him: "Leave me alone, I cannot take any more. I feel bullied by you. This is not the first time you have harassed me". He ends the meeting and arranges his executive coaching session.

We put "bullying and harassment" into the Pitfall and I ask him what he was doing too much of to have it labelled "bullying or harassment". He knew immediately, "I was being action-oriented", he said. So, I summarized, "if action oriented was your core quality and bullying or harassment is your Pitfall, what is your Challenge"? Again he knew almost immediately. "Going at her pace". And of course, his Allergy is individuals who never get things done (no action). We now plan for the future and I coach him in how to stay action oriented and proceed at the pace of the slowest member to ensure the individual and the team is with him. He saw the sense: the poor member of staff was exhausted, had no break for nearly three hours and felt compelled to remain engaged when she needed to get away. For Jeremy not to end up in his Pitfall he had to learn how to go at the speed of others, not just engaging with his own high levels of stamina and energy.

It would have been easy for me (his coach) to lecture him on the ills of bullying or harassment but the Theory of Core Qualities gave him an understanding and insight into this behaviour that does not just concentrate on the negative. It places the negative (the Pitfall) in a much larger picture where the weaknesses are seen as related to the strengths. This does not justify what happens in the Pitfall but it makes it more easily understood and accepted when placed in the wider context.

1. Decisive people (core quality) will be allergic to passivity.
2. Empathetic people (core quality) will have an allergy to selfishness.
3. Loyal individuals will be allergic to betrayal or deceit.

In brief the model looks like this:

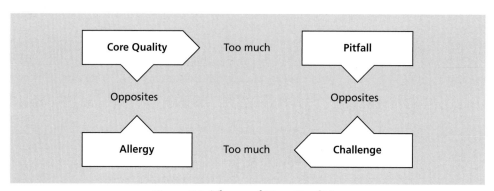

Figure 7.2: Theory of Core Qualities

1. The Pitfall is too much of the Core Quality.
2. The Challenge is the positive opposite of the Pitfall.
3. The Allergy is too much of the challenge.
4. The Core Quality is the positive opposite of the Allergy.

Exercise

Go to Appendix 13 and see if you can fill in the four areas of the quadrant for yourself.

Conclusion

...The focus of feedback (negative or positive) is to facilitate learning...

Giving and receiving feedback are both demanding processes. They take some courage and a good deal of skill. The focus of feedback (negative or positive) is to facilitate learning. The best learning is a process of: practice, feedback, practice, feedback, practice, feedback etc.

Example

If you were her executive coach, how might you work with Jane to help her be more open to feedback? Jane is clearly terrified of negative feedback. Twice now you have given her feedback on her interpersonal style as a manager and both times she has become very upset and distressed. You do not want her to go through such pain and anguish every time you give negative feedback, especially since her reaction seems out of proportion to the feedback you give. However, you want to retain the right to give her feedback to help her learn. You are wondering what you can do to help Jane hear and use feedback more positively.

Review And Discussion

1. Are you clear about how feedback is connected to learning?

2. Can you see the connections between giving and receiving feedback now and our past history of giving and receiving feedback?
3. Do you have a clear method and approach to giving feedback that helps another person learn (a framework)?
4. Can you now be open and free to listen to feedback (especially critical or negative feedback) as a way of learning?

Chapter 8

Coachee Skill 3: Learning Realistic Self-Evaluation

Introduction

Evaluation refers to the process of assessing the competence of our work in terms of its effectiveness and the desired outcomes. Clearly this is a central aspect of executive coaching. As we mentioned in our discussion on developmental stages in the learning process, the aim of professional learning is to develop a reliable 'internal coach or supervisor' who can evaluate our own competence as we go along. Evaluation includes the provision of ongoing feedback in executive coaching sessions and the overall evaluation of your work at certain points. We see evaluation as an ongoing process in executive coaching that, at its best, is a collaborative process with clearly agreed goals and milestones that are defined and stipulated along the way.

...The secret is to develop the capacity to receive feedback...

One of the biggest challenges for any professional is learning realistic self-evaluation. Most of the people we meet in coaching relationships are very hard on themselves and tend to criticize all they do in a very negative and disqualifying manner. This is doubly difficult because a) they do not recognize what they actually do effectively and where their points of development realistically may be; and b) they also tend to overreact to any suggestions made by their coach which they may interpret as a complete negation of themselves. If you get into a process of this kind, it will be very difficult for anyone to give you any useful feedback! The secret is to develop the capacity to receive feedback, listen to it carefully and evaluate it for yourself and use it as the basis for further learning and setting further learning goals.

One of the aims of executive coaching is for the coachee to develop an internal coach/supervisor that is well balanced, well informed and realistic about goal setting. What is important is to be very clear about the goals or outcomes you want to achieve and then look at the criteria by which you will assess these.

Specific criteria will, of course, be related to your particular area of work but it may be helpful to look at some general guidelines here.

1. What is your goal or aim in this piece of work?
2. How will you know that you have achieved a successful outcome?
3. What specific behavioural criteria will you use to assess your performance?
4. What do you most appreciate about what you did?
5. What would you do differently next time?
6. What have you learned from this particular analysis?
7. What is your next area for development?

Self-evaluation can involve different areas. Gilbert and Sills (1999) describe three 'lenses' through which evaluation can take place: a) a focus on micro skills; b) a focus on a particular session or task; and c) a focus on development over time. We will discuss each of these in turn to show how they can enhance and build realistic self-evaluation of work.

Evaluating Micro skills

This involves an interaction-by-interaction analysis of an interaction with an individual or segment of an interaction (eg., an appraisal or a team meeting) with a view to identifying effective and non-effective interventions and practicing alternatives. An audio or video recording is of particular help in this micro-analytic process.

Exercise

Choose an intervention that you considered effective (an appraisal you led, a project you have been involved in, a difficult relationship you handled well etc) and reflect on this in terms of the individual's immediate (and subsequent) responses. How can you tell (by change of energy, intensity of affect etc.) that you have 'reached' this person?

Exercise

Choose a point in the work where you were particularly aware that you had a choice and could have made a number of different responses/interventions. Focus on the choice point and recall what you were thinking at that time.

What other options were you considering?

What led you to make this particular choice (for example, employee considerations, contextual factors, strategic considerations, which made you feel it was best or because you were scared of conflict and therefore chose the line of least resistance)?

Do you consider that your choice led to an effective outcome? If so, why? If not, why not?

How does the choice of this particular intervention relate to your managerial values?

What might you wish to experiment with differently in the future?

Practice a few alternatives. (After Gilbert and Evans 2000, p52).

...exposure to the feedback of others is helpful in developing realistic self-evaluation...

Role-play is a particularly useful way of practicing alternative interventions. In this way you can experiment with new options and get immediate feedback from your executive coach about the effectiveness of your interventions. You can begin to widen your repertoire of micro skills and get immediate feedback to evaluate your new points of learning. Such exposure to the feedback of others is helpful in developing realistic self-evaluation and can help us to begin to 'see ourselves as others see us' rather than hanging onto unrealistic self-assessments.

Evaluating A Coaching Session

Here the evaluation will relate to a completed session or task. Again you will first be looking at whether you have achieved your overall goal or aim in this piece of work. As an example of a sessional evaluation, we will provide some questions to consider that could arise in a coaching session.

1. Did you and your executive coach mutually agree a clear and manageable contract for the session?
2. In other words, did you negotiate specific objectives, and explicit and measurable goals?
3. Was this contract completed by the end of the session?
4. Did you clarify your expectations for the session?
5. Did the session allow for an honest and open exchange?
6. Did the executive coach provide both support and challenge?

7. Was feedback specific, respectful and related to the contract?
8. Did the session provide a balance of action and reflection?
9. Was the atmosphere warm and collaborative?
10. Did you experiment with new options/ideas with the support of the coach?
11. Did you have fun in the learning process?

(After Gilbert and Sills, 1999).

These questions are based on some of the findings that highlight the qualities inherent in effective coaching. You can draw up a similar list for any task in terms of the standards for that piece of work and then use these criteria as a guideline for realistic self-evaluation. Vagueness about the criteria we are using for self-assessment can encourage falling back into self-criticism and self-depreciating comments that have very little basis in the reality of our efforts. The question remains: What are the specific criteria by which we are evaluating our performance? And are these realistic and achievable?

Here is a short checklist from Gilbert and Sills (1999) which will help you review an executive coaching session quickly:

1. What was your contract and have you met it?
2. What have you found most useful from your coaching?
3. What do you want more of from your coach?
4. What do you want less of from your coach?
5. What is the next developmental edge for you?

Evaluating Development Over Time

...will also include questions about your overall satisfaction in the job...

Sometimes, in executive coaching, we wish to review our development over the past year or our progress in a particular job over a specified period of time. This means taking a longer view of aims and goals and achievements (and of goals not realized). Such a review will involve a discussion of particular goals related to your performance but will also include questions about your overall satisfaction in the job. Some questions that might help you reflect on your motivation are:

1. Do I enjoy what I am doing?
2. What is my primary motivation for doing this work?
3. Does my job give me satisfaction?
4. Am I learning what I need to support myself well?
5. Have I made a choice of career that suits my abilities and proclivities?
6. What am I most passionate about in this area of work?

Coachees are well advised to agree learning goals with their executive coaching for a period of time - usually for the next few months - so that they have an overall learning plan. Such goals may be:

1. To focus on the underlying values that drive my behaviour.
2. To broaden and increase my repertoire of skills especially in facilitating team meetings.
3. To firm up on appraisal skills.
4. To hone my presentation skills.
5. To improve the clarity of my communications, especially when written or sent by email.

In this way, as a coachee, you will not only have a contract for a particular session but will also have an overall learning goal for the year that relates to your ongoing development as a professional. These longer-term goals could be reviewed every three months to assess your progress and focus anew on your growing edges as a practitioner. Longer-term contracts can also cover new areas that you wish to be introduced to by your executive coach and to receive guidance in developing and exploring.

Executive contracts are often made for three months, six months or a year at a time so at the last session of each agreed time allotment the coaching contract could be used to review this level of your learning and development with a view to looking forward to the next phase. Sometimes this may involve moving on to another executive coach with a different way of working or with a different skills area so that you can be challenged in a new way.

Shaming Interferes With Learning

In both giving and receiving feedback as well as in self evaluation and evaluations/assessment by others, particular attention needs to be paid to what would militate against these being used effectively. One major block to both is the issue of shame.

Shame is a process that can interfere with learning. When we experience shame, we want to hide away and protect ourselves rather than enter into dialogue. If we start to experience shame, we may hesitate to admit to ourselves or others that we need help or support in learning. Many people have had shaming experiences in the course of their schooling where they have been humiliated for 'not knowing'; consequently they may have learnt to hide their needs and shut down on their natural right to be informed and ask for information. Trust may have been severely undermined in relation to the learning environment. As coachees, we may bring a history of this kind to the coaching relationship. This kind of educational history has often left people believing that there is only one 'right' way of doing things and that lies in the hands of the 'authority' and that different options, points of view and ways of doing things are not acceptable. It is important to raise fears and doubts of this kind in order to have a good coaching relationship (see Gilbert and Evans, 2000 for a discussion of shame in supervision). We recommend a coaching contract in which mutual respect for each other's points of view is a ground rule and where it is clearly understood that this is a co-operative relationship!

Kaufman (1992) in his exploration of shame writes of the mutuality that is central to our feeling secure in a real relationship with another. "The bond which ties two individuals together forms an interpersonal bridge between them" (Kaufmann 1992:13). In this process of mutuality, we can permit ourselves to receive respect and valuing from the other. Such an atmosphere of trust provides a facilitative environment for learning to take place. This interpersonal bridge is built on certain expectations of a relationship, which will be influenced by our past experience of rewarding relationships in general and will, of course, be significantly impacted by the respectful approach of people to us in the present.

If someone ridicules us and our struggles, the interpersonal bridge will be broken by this rupture in the relationship. If this has happened to us repeatedly in past learning situations, we may be reluctant to open up to new learning in the present, especially where our need is great and we feel a reluctance to admit to vulnerability and the need for help. However, should we experience shame in a coaching relationship, however inadvertent this may be on the part of the coach, it will be important to open up the discussion so that you can mend the rupture in the relationship together for further learning to occur. Someone who does not know our history may sometimes put ideas into a form of words that we find difficult because of our past experience. Such misunderstandings are good to discuss and clarify otherwise this will stand in the way of further learning until the trust has been re-established in the relationship. Kaufman (1992) speaks of this process as healing the interpersonal bridge between people; this can serve as a powerful reparative process in the present especially where shame-based learning has occurred in the past. We can then move forward with the learning process.

Conclusion

...evaluate yourself and your competencies realistically, without being too positive or too negative on yourself...

In this section, our hope is that you will be able to evaluate yourself and your competencies realistically, without being too positive or too negative on yourself. Self-evaluation is a key to progress. Combined with your coach's evaluation, and the evaluations of significant others, it becomes a marvellous tool for learning.

Examples

Harry is consistently over optimistic in his evaluations of his skills, his competencies and his capabilities. Eleanor, his executive coach is surprised with the gap between her evaluation of him and his own. She is wondering how she should tackle this difference and where the real problem lies. As an executive coachee what might your advice be for her?

Jenny continually puts herself down. When Eleanor asks her to evaluate herself the negatives come first. She might then reluctantly admit to some positive attributes or skills usually only after prompting from Eleanor. Eleanor wonders what she can do to help Jenny be more realistic and balanced in her self evaluations. How might you advise Eleanor from your position as executive coachee?

Review And Discussion

1. Do you consider yourself able to be realistic about evaluating yourself and your work? Is your tendency to be more positive than negative, or vice-versa?
2. Do you have clear criteria against which you evaluate yourself professionally?
3. Can you see the beginnings of "an internal coach/supervisor" that monitors your work while you are doing it and evaluates what you are doing realistically?
4. Can you see how your evaluation of yourself can be set within a developmental process – where you have come from and where you are going?

Chapter 9

Coachee Skill 4: Learning How To Reflect

Introduction

Humans have the ability to reflect. Our language is replete with words and phrases showing our propensity to reflect: "I thought about what you said….I'll mull it over and we'll talk tomorrow… what do you think about what he did? Why did you do that? I caught myself saying…. Let me think some more about it…." We not only act but also then think about what we have done; and we can even think about our thinking on what we have done. Reflection is a crucial element in learning. Not being able to reflect means being condemned to repeating actions over and over again, to living out the scripts of others, and to living out received wisdom and learning that is handed to us but which never has been owned by us. For that is what reflection is: the ability to examine, to observe, to look at, to review, to evaluate, to interrogate, to assess, to question and to own our own thinking.

…the ability to reflect has much to do with our past and our experience of prior reflection…

Reflection is a sophisticated skill. Like learning itself, the ability to reflect has much to do with our past and our experience of prior reflection, as well as our personality, environment and the people who surround us.

What Is Reflection?

The actual word "reflection" comes from a Latin root meaning "to bend back, to stand apart from, to stand outside of". In reflection, we take a step back and look at what we or others have done. Reflection means stepping back from an experience or an event so that I can gain a new perspectives on what I have done.

Here are some definitions of reflection:

1. "Reflection is an active, persistent and careful consideration of any belief or supposed form of knowledge in the light of the grounds that support it and the future conclusions to which it leads" (Dewey, 1933).
2. "Reflection can be defined as thinking and feeling activities in which individuals engage to explore their experiences in order to lead to new understandings and appreciations" (Boud, Keogh and Walker, 1985: 19).
3. "Reflection is a process by which I interrogate my own thoughts, feelings and actions".
4. "Reflection is the ability to create meaning and conceptualization from experience and the potentiality to look at things other than as they are" (Brockbank and McGill, 1998).
5. "Reflexivity is the intention to examine one's actions, active and critical inquiry, openness to alternatives and willing to be vulnerable to try out new ideas" (Neufeldt, 1999).

A number of areas are covered by these definitions:

1. Reflection is an "internal" activity. I harness my thoughts and feelings to consider, to think about what has happened. I go inside to access my capacity to review what I have done or what has happened. Reflection starts with being able to stop doing and begin thinking about what has transpired.
2. The purpose of the activity is to hold "up to the light", to allow it to speak to me so that I can learn from it.

3. Reflection is a process of examination, inquiry, self-interrogation where I ask questions of the activity itself. Why did this happen? Why did I do that? Why did that person respond in that way? Why do I keep getting into these situations?
4. Reflection is a way of making sense of, giving meaning to events and experiences. It is a meaning-making facility that helps me understand from a number of perspectives. Widening reflectivity means widening the meaning –making frameworks from which I work.
5. Reflection is not just a rational event – it is an emotional experience as well as a rational one.

From this understanding I can then look at alternatives, other ways of thinking or doing.

Schon (1983; 1987) talks about two types of reflection: reflection-in-action and reflection-on-action. The first is that part of ourselves that observes and reflects on what we are doing as we are doing it - what Bolton calls "the hawk in your mind constantly circling over your head watching and advising on your actions – while you are practicing" (2001:15). Casement (1985) coined the term "internal supervisor" to capture this type of reflection within the area of psychotherapy. As we engage with our work, we become our own supervisor, monitoring, thinking, evaluating, and assessing what is going on. It is a way of making sense of what is happening as it is happening. The second kind of reflection is the more luxurious reflection-on-action where we stop activities and intentionally put ourselves into a stance of reflection. We are provided with time, space, safety and attention to focus on and think about our experiences. Executive coaching mostly uses this second type of reflection but with experience comes the ability to reflect-in-action.

Exercise

Using some of the definitions above could you take 10 minutes to reflect on something that has happened to you recently? It could be a personal or professional experience. Take notes of what is happening to you during this process.

Learning Reflection

...Facing a problem makes individuals or groups "ripe for reflection"...

How can we move from a non-reflective stance to a reflexive position? Can we learn how to reflect? An external event is not always needed to engender reflection but for many people (especially those not used to or skilled in reflection) an external happening often propels them into reflection. Facing a problem makes individuals or groups "ripe for reflection". Uncertainty, confusion and surprise are often emotional pathways to helping us reconsider and think through what we have never thought through before. Wake-up calls, high-wire moments, shocks and traumas – all are potential triggers for processes of reflection. They impel us to wonder why, to question, to review our old way of thinking which is inadequate to encompass this new event.

The "internal" requirements that facilitate our reflections are:

1. Openness and open-mindedness. Rokeach (1960) defines open-mindedness as "the extent to which a person can receive, evaluate, and act on relevant information received from outside on its own intrinsic merits unencumbered by irrelevant factors in the situation arising from within the person or from outside" (p. 57). Being honest with oneself, being open to "whatever truth comes through the door", being courageous enough to stay with the facts all greatly assist reflection.

2. Invention and imagination ie., the ability to go beyond our own psychological boundaries and parameters and permit ourselves to think other possibilities.
3. The ability to stop, be still, recall – get distance from.
4. Suspending evaluation, become non-evaluative until you have had time to observe and take in all the information.
5. Listening to self and others allows you to make sense of what is happening.
6. Respecting intuition and feelings as guides toward understanding.
7. Thinking as a "beginner".
8. Looking for other meanings eg., how might others make sense of this?
9. Widening one's perspective.
10. Being vulnerable.
11. Befriending the unfamiliar and the uncomfortable.
12. Being emotionally aware – of what is happening to ourselves and to others.

Blocks To Reflection

...Some people cannot be "still" either physically or psychologically...

Blocks to reflection can also be internal or external. Being stressed, tired, exhausted makes reflection very difficult – the mind is too weary or the opposite, too preoccupied. In our "world of high speed", it is often impossible to get quality reflection time. Some people cannot be "still" either physically or psychologically, again making reflection difficult. Perhaps we have to move more today towards "reflection-in-action" where the very speed of life means we need to learn to contemplate quickly as we engage in activity. Our society's glorification of "action" and "outcomes" can often result in poor support for reflective activity because "the point of it" is not billable or rewarded; organizations do not build it into work time. Personality types may also affect the need and the ability to reflect and whether one is introverted or extroverted may indicate ease or not with reflection in action and reflection on action.

Facilitating Reflection

How can we facilitate our own reflection and the reflection of others? A number of authors have made suggestions. Kline (1999) presents the "Ten Components of a Thinking Environment" which, together, help us learn how to think for ourselves. The 10 components are:

1. Attention: listening with respect, interest and fascination.
2. Incisive Questions: asking questions that facilitate reflection.
3. Equality: treating others as equal thinking peers.
4. Appreciation: looking with eyes that see the positive.
5. Ease: slowing down and freeing from rush or urgency.
6. Encouragement – moving beyond competition.
7. Feelings: allowing ourselves to feel.
8. Information – finding out as much as possible.
9. Place – an environment that says "you matter".
10. Diversity – adding quality because of difference.

There is no doubt that questions are a key way in which to facilitate reflection. The right question jolts, goes to the heart of the matter, surprises, makes the listener realize that their solutions to date no longer work with this issue. Reflective questions lead to insight. We look for "trigger questions as a way of promoting reflective learning" (Levy, 1980).

One way to facilitate reflection is helping learners find their own voice. Voicing reflections helps encourage reflection – there is some truth in the statement that I do not know what I know until I have said it, or written it down. Giving feedback is another way of helping individuals begin to reflect.

Individuals learn to reflect at ever deepening levels when they:

1. Learn how to be empathetic and see events from other perspectives.
2. Are confused in their thinking.
3. Begin to look at the consequences of their behaviour.
4. Monitor and articulate their feelings.
5. Are challenged to look at what they are doing and why they are doing it.
6. Ask incisive questions.
7. Create connections to others.
8. Specifically go out to meet others who are different and think differently.
9. Are shocked.
10. Move towards authenticity and congruence.
11. Begin to self-disclose.
12. Build up their thinking skills.
13. Stop.
14. Are prepared to experiment.
15. Use counselling, training or courses to review their way of reflecting.
16. Are allowed to change roles.
17. Befriend the uncomfortable and unfamiliar.
18. Put themselves in challenging (stretching) situations.
19. Live with groups that think differently.

...there is no doubt that helping people reflect in groups is a very valuable way of helping individuals...

Reflection is too important to be left to chance. Too much depends on it to hope that it might be picked up during the journey of life. Rather, it seems wiser to teach or facilitate how to reflect, so that individuals and groups can be assured of having such a precious commodity. While facilitating reflection here has been defined as an individual task, there is no doubt that helping people reflect in groups is a very valuable way of helping individuals.

Five Levels Of Reflection

The following section suggests that there are levels of reflection open to us and that each new level allows us to encompass wider considerations into our reflection.

Level 1: Reflection Focuses On How Events Affect Me, Alone.

Level 1reflection is a very elementary stage of reflection. It is the reflective process that does not include anyone else other than self. My welfare and myself become the centre around which my reflections occur. This level of reflection is close to what Lawrence Kohlberg depicted as his first level of moral reasoning. For Kohlberg, moral reasoning at level 1 was solely focused on how an action affected me physically, and me alone. At this level of reflection, individuals think very simply and in very discrete categories. In many ways, it is an unreflective stance in life. An individual does not stop to think about why they do what they do. Kegan (1994) has some instances of this kind of thinking:

Judge: Tom, how can you steal from people who trust you?

Tom: Because, Your Honour, it's very difficult to steal from people who don't trust you.

Judge: Billy, why do you continually steal money from banks?

Billy: Because, Your Honour, that is where the money is.

…We can ask too much of a person regarding their ability to reflect…

In neither case is the defendant answering the judge's question but is answering as far as his limited reflection will allow him - which is confusing for the judge because he is hoping that some insight at a different level of reflection will occur (eg., on how your actions affect people who trust you or, in the case of Billy, some awareness of his motivation on robbing banks). We can ask too much of a person regarding their ability to reflect making it important to match our interventions to their level of reflective ability.

Reflection, at this level, is connected to personal safety and to self-preservation, and events in life and in the world are considered insofar as they affect me, my life and my safety.

Exercise

What would Level 1 reflection in an executive coachee look like? Can you think of an example from your own life or work that indicates Level 1 reflection?

Level 2: Reflection On How It Affects Me In My Core Relationships

The mental equipment that people at Level 2 bring to reflection includes not just reflection on themselves but others in their group. Kohlberg called this Level 3 in his model of moral reasoning: morality, which centres around what my group finds right or wrong. This is group thinking about what is held dear by the group and the individual does not question or really reflect on the rightness or wrongness, goodness or badness of such behaviour. Hence, the difficulty of asking teenagers to be disloyal to their group – it is too much to ask.

This unreflectiveness can invade all kinds of loyalties. Many religious people faithfully follow their religious leaders without reflecting on whether they are right or wrong. Loyalty to groups (whether religious, political, educational, industrial) can stymie individual thinking and reflection. Many organizations reward this kind of "loyalty" which takes away thinking and reflection from the individual and places it with authority figures. This dilemma is resolved by dependence on the group or institution or organization, which brings confidence, loyalty, and commitment but keeps learning restricted. Level 2 reflection and thinking will use terms like:

1. If you are my friend then you will stand by me (irrespective of what I do).
2. If you loved me then you would…
3. No surrender.
4. My country, right or wrong.
5. It's them… or us.
6. You are with me or against me.

Reflection (ie., thinking about and examining events) will happen only in the light of the values, norms and criteria of the group to which I feel loyal. This level explains why highly religious and indeed, highly idealistic, individuals can involve themselves in all sorts of horrendous and hurtful actions despite their deep religious beliefs.

Effective reflection cannot happen where we have to deal with major issues of rejection or isolation. An example of someone in this reflective mode is a young Muslim worker whose environment does not support reflecting critically on what it means to be a Muslim. Reflecting in this way can easily become a danger. If the young person allows himself/herself to become critically reflective the result could be either at odds with their community or result in outright rejection by the community. In this instance (and it can equally apply to other religions, certain political systems and authoritarian organizations) the environment does not support critical reflection because the consequences might be too dangerous for the reflector and the community (eg., that the person might have to leave the group).

Exercise

What might a coachee at Level 2 look like? Can you spot reflection at Level 2 in your own work?

Level 3: Reflection At The Level Of Inquiry, Of Abstraction, Of Principles And Of Human Relationships.

...someone will actively and independently consider an action wrong rather than look for an indirect way of explaining it...

Level 3 reflexivity goes beneath action to motivation, to effects on others, to abstract principles. The difference at this level is that someone will actively and independently consider an action wrong rather than look for an indirect way of explaining it (eg., I cannot vote for you because I think you are not right for the job rather than, I will not vote for you because I will not be at the meeting). Level 3 reflection is about authenticity, congruence with myself and adherence to principles I see as good and worthwhile. It demands a good degree of self-awareness, insight into my reasons for doing things, knowing myself, and a good degree of empathy around how this might affect others. For people at Level 3 reflexivity, it would be very difficult to get involved in mindless violence (go out on a weekend, get drunk and start a fight). Level 3 reflection means that I have come up with principles that guide my life and so there is a certain amount of self-authorization in life.

Level 3 reflectors might use statements like:

1. I won't do it because I believe it is wrong.
2. My own conclusion is that...
3. I have thought about it and have come to the conclusion that it is right to do that because...
4. I know the group believes this is the way forward but I would like to disagree... other principles are involved.

At Level 3, individuals are independent in their own right and can begin to think for themselves. They are, therefore, able to reflect in a widening circle of what is good, worthwhile, and valuable in its own right (not because it is connected to me or to my group).

Example

Isobel comes to her executive coaching session upset about what happened at work. Her boss insisted that she give the outsourcing tender to a company he has dealt with and with whom he has good relationships. This action of his is not only against company policy but, as the person who organized and chose the suitable application, it is against Isobel's choice of the best candidate. She likes her boss, but what is happening is against her own sense of justice and integrity. However she feels torn between wanting to keep her job and good relationship with her boss on one hand and, on the other hand, her sense of justice and authenticity.

Exercise

What might an executive coachee at Level 3 look like? Again, can you see examples of Level 3 reflection in yourself?

Level 4: Reflection That Connects Across Categories.

...They know the inner logic of their own mind...

People at level 4 reflexivity know how they think and construct experience. They are aware of the categories and assumptions that underlie their ways of constructing meaning in the world and are aware of how they organize their thinking, feelings and actions. They know the inner logic of their own mind. They know the basis of their thinking and their principles are not fixed or final but constantly changing. The principles that guide them are principles that engage them to their environment – they are connected to others in many ways and to the world in which they live. In the light of the above, they understand parameters and boundaries and create and re-create roles and relationships. These are new sets of ideas eg., ideas about ideas, relating to my relationships, reviewing the presuppositions that keep me where I am. This is a stage of development where the individual has moved from belonging to a group and adhering to its dictates to a mind-set that includes ideas of self-actualization, equality and wholeness that connects him/her to others and the world.

At level 4, we re-construct the very principles by which we give meaning to things. People at Level 4 question their own way of thinking and the way of thinking of others and make statements like:

1. I know I am making general statements when I say...
2. That conclusion doesn't follow from those statements.
3. I now know why I think that way...
4. Having been brought up in my family in this context, I begin to understand why...
5. Yes, that is an assumption I make.

These statements show the ability to go beneath the thinking to question the thinking itself (the premises on which it is based). At this Level 4, we can begin to see that what we often take as "truth" actually derives from social background, family, upbringing and parochial training. It is replete with assumptions.

Example

Leonard wants to know why he thinks the way he does about his colleagues at work. He is so critical, so judgmental that he surprises himself how quickly he moves into evaluation mode before giving a person a chance. He has noticed that this is a pattern in the way he works with both colleagues and his own boss. His executive coach, Jeff, spends time with him and they discover that he does to himself what he does to others. There is so much he cannot stand in himself; he is so unaccepting of who he is that he continually notices the negatives well before any positives. His reflections bring him into looking at the assumptions behind his thinking.

Exercise

Again, as above, you might want to look at what an executive coachee at Level 4 looks like. Are there areas of your own reflection that fall within this category?

Level 5 Reflexivity: Based On Difference And Diversity

...using conflict as an enriching experience, on believing in multiple selves, on using flexibility at a high level...

This level of reflectiveness, which Kegan calls post-modern, is based on the seeing the richness and value of diversity (rather than simply the tolerance or acceptance of it), on using conflict as an enriching experience, on believing in multiple selves, on using flexibility at a high level, on believing in relationships as the very source of learning, on transforming from "doing" to "being". Kegan speculates that this level is not accessible to those under 40 where interdependence and synergy become the order of the day.

Statements that people at this level of reflexivity might use are:

1. Yes, it's not in our economic interest short term but it is best for the world in the long-term.
2. Can we begin to think about the debts of poorer countries?
3. Asylum seekers living in our communities often bring an interesting mix of challenges and creative solutions.

Reflection at Level 5 is wide: it considers the value or worth of events in as far as they affect the world community rather than the narrow interests of individuals or individual countries.

Example

Justine is worried about the effects the work of her Company has on the environment. She has reached a stage where she can no longer remain quiet about what, in her estimation, is a gross misuse of environmental resources. In executive coaching she is looking at what is an appropriate way to help her give this feedback to the Company in a way that might help them listen and change.

Exercise

What does an executive coachee at Level 5 look like? How could you integrate more Level 5 reflection into your own life and work?

Review And Discussion

1. Can you describe what reflection means?
2. What are the deepening levels of reflection and could you say how a person might move to deeper levels?
3. How might you become more reflective?
4. What blocks reflection (your own, in particular) and how might you unblock it?
5. What do you think might happen in coaching if a coachee was at a different (higher?) level of reflection than the coach?

Chapter 10

Coachee Skill 5: Learning Emotional Awareness

Introduction

Emotions are often the forgotten side of coaching and learning. Learning is emotion-based. Executive coaching is an emotional experience. How we deal with the emotional side of executive coaching relationships, of feedback in coaching, of assessment, evaluation and executive coaching reports - not to mention disputes, conflicts and disagreement - is often not even considered on the coaching agenda. Weisinger (1998) writes about "emotional fallout" when feedback is delivered destructively. Emotional intelligence helps us deal with many of these issues.

In general, women are more emotionally aware than men (Orme, 2001). So men, in particular, have to pay attention to their ability to tune into feelings - their own and those of others - and take appropriate action. We know also that feelings, and the ability to express them, is connected to upbringing and the lessons gleaned from our environment and upbringing (eg., "big boys don't cry"), and can be connected to culture and race. Some cultures are more accepting of expressing feelings than others which are less so, eg., the British have a reputation of having a "stiff upper lip".

Emotional Intelligence

...Feelings help us stay in touch with ourselves and our values...

Goleman (1996) in his now famous book "Emotional Intelligence" defines emotional intelligence (or EI) as the "capacity for recognising our feelings and those of others, for motivating ourselves and for managing emotions well in ourselves and in our relationships". Mayer and Salovey (1997) define it as "a learned ability to monitor one's own and other's feelings and emotions, to discriminate among them and to use this information to guide one's thinking and actions". Feelings help us stay in touch with ourselves and our values. They help us make decisions and facilitate us moving on (the word emotion comes from the Latin word "to move"). Emotional language allows us to put our feelings into words and hence be able to deal with them more effectively and constructively. Weisinger (1998) suggests four building blocks to emotional literacy:

1. The ability to accurately perceive, appraise and express emotion.
2. The ability to access or generate feelings on demand when they can facilitate understanding of yourself or another person.
3. The ability to understand emotions and use the knowledge that derives from them.
4. The ability to regulate emotions.

Ways Of Managing Emotions

Individuals have different ways of handling and managing their feelings. Some of these are:

1. Being aware of feelings and expressing them appropriately.
2. Not in touch with feelings – they come out in other ways rather than appropriate expression (I get angry with my team rather than with my boss).
3. Engulfed with feelings (eg., road rage, violence etc).
4. Emotions expressed somatically (they come out in physical reactions – pain in the body, headaches etc).

Carl Rogers talked about seven levels of feelings:

1. Feelings are not owned, not recognized, not connected to.
2. Feelings are owned but talked about as in the past.
3. Feelings are described rather than felt.
4. Feelings are owned but externalized (well, one would feel angry).
5. Feelings are expressed as present.
6. There is a flow of feelings in the here and now.
7. There is access to full feelings as they happen and ability to express them appropriately.

Exercise

Use Rogers' Seven Levels of Feelings to see where you are in respect to owning and expressing certain feelings. Look at the list in Appendix 11 to help you.

Exercise

How in touch are you with your feelings?

Exercise

See: Goleman's Emotional Competency Framework (Appendix 10 outlines the Emotional Competency Framework).

Here are some processes that might help you to get in touch with feelings and be able to act appropriately on them:

...Are there some feelings you are more comfortable with than others...

1. Recognize the importance of feelings.
2. Give feelings permission to be.
3. Acknowledge feelings.
4. Realize there are no good or bad feelings – feelings are feelings.
5. Listen to and observe your body – it might let you know about feelings.
6. Every so often stop and finish the sentence, "Just now, I am feeling…".
7. Listen to your feelings – what are they saying to you?
8. Listen to the feelings of other people – ask yourself, what is this person feeling now?
9. Put another person's feelings into words (not necessarily for them but for yourself), eg., "This person is feeling…".
10. Are there some feelings you are more comfortable with than others (some people deny certain feelings eg., feeling hurt, or angry, or "full of rage")?
11. Can you distinguish within feelings (there is a continuum from mild irritation to fury with feelings such as anger somewhere along the continuum)?
12. Can you distinguish between feelings (hurt, resentment, anger, sadness)? Some people get feelings mixed up regarding intensity or duration.
13. Distinguish between thoughts, feelings and actions.
14. Can you take time between feeling and doing? Some people are very impulsive with feelings and do not take a measured response which, at times, can help.
15. Begin to monitor how your body reacts to certain feelings (when I feel scared – there are butterflies in my stomach, my mouth dries up, I cannot focus, my palms are sweaty).

16. Have a look at a list of feeling words in Appendix 11. Which of these feelings do you find easy to acknowledge and express, which ones are difficult for you to accept and articulate appropriately?
17. Are there some feelings you "privatize" ie., you pull them inside yourself and do not let them be expressed eg., some people do this with anger (once privatized, it can then become depression).
18. Have a look at layers of feelings (guilt and shame can come together or anger and hurt and guilt all get mingled).

...Sometimes we have to deal with a backlog of feelings...

Sometimes we have to deal with a backlog of feelings ie., feelings that have remained unexpressed for some time eg., loss and bereavement can be triggered by a present event (we lay what someone referred to as "gunpowder trails" where an occurrence in the present can trigger an explosion from the past).

Ostell, Beverstock and Wright (1999) suggest some principles on managing emotions that are helpful for coaches and coachees:

Principle 1: Deal with the emotional reaction before attempting to resolve the problem

1. Engage the rational only when the level of emotion is reduced.
2. Reflective statements are very helpful.
3. Apologize if appropriate.
4. Acknowledge the feeling.
5. Stay with it as long as is needed.

Principle 2: Avoid behaviours and trigger words that heighten adverse emotional reactions.

1. Some words heighten the emotion rather than reduce it eg., words such as stupid, worthless, etc.
2. Unconstructive mood matching (eg., anger for anger, sarcasm for sarcasm). I respond in the same mood as you.
3. A type of confrontation that simply disparages another's emotional experience: eg., "don't be childish, grow up, getting upset won't help, you are over reacting".

Principle 3: Employ behaviours likely to dissipate adverse emotional reactions.

1. Empathy to indicate understanding.
2. Giving permission to express emotion through active, nonjudgmental listening.
3. Normalising the emotion eg., "it's okay to feel that way".
4. "Time out" to recompose and continue at a later date.
5. Giving ideas that might help resolve the issues.
6. Empathize with the person.

Principle 4: Recognize differences between emotions

Different emotions tend to be provoked and sustained by different ways of thinking eg., three employees who have failed to get a promotion:

1. One feels angry: violation of rights ("I should have been...").
2. One feels anxious: anticipates negative consequences ("I'm stuck here").
3. One feels depressed: helplessness and self-blame ("It's my fault, I am not good enough.").

Some suggested responses:

103

1. To the angry - apologize.
2. To the anxious - the consequences are manageable and may not be as bad as you imagine.
3. To the depressed: getting some control and power through new skills: "You have the resources to help yourself and with support you can access these resources".

The more deeply these emotions are felt, the more professional the help required.

Principle 5: Where appropriate, attempt to find a solution to the underlying problem.

Unless the underlying problem is dealt with, the negative emotional response is likely to re-occur.

1. It may be enough to have time for emotional expression and to feel understood.
2. Nondirective approach: facilitating the person to find their own solution.
3. Directive methods: giving advice, problem solving, offering possible options.

Principle 6: Actively learn to accept reality

1. Some situations cannot be solved (eg., loss and death).
2. Some cannot be resolved because of others (redundancy, neighbours, etc).

Some principles that help us in addressing emotions in the executive coaching relationship:

... distinguish between everyday emotional reaction (reactions to missed deadlines, bonus at work, etc) and emotional problems of a more complicated nature...

1. Deal with disruptive emotional behaviour.
2. Important to distinguish between everyday emotional reaction (reactions to missed deadlines, bonus at work, etc) and emotional problems of a more complicated nature (PTSD, chronic depression, paranoia).
3. Help each of us find ways of better managing situations and our reactions to them instead of trying to diagnose problems.
4. Refer for expert help when necessary.

Conclusion

Learning "emotional literacy" will help you deal more effectively with the kinds of issues that arise in your work and in your coaching. Emotions are not just internal reactions but connect us - in ways we sometimes cannot even imagine - to life and others. Far from being simply distractions to tolerate or accept passively, feelings become the "inner rudder" of our lives, personally and professionally.

Example

Joel is simply not in touch with his feelings. When his executive coach, Muriel, asks him how he feels about events at work (he has just been overlooked for a major promotion) he shrugs his shoulders and replies from a thinking rather than a feeling perspective. She has noticed that he is overly rational and reasonable but misses picking up emotions and feelings in his relationships with others. She wonders how she can coach him to be more emotionally literate.

Review And Discussion

1. What is the importance of being aware of emotions within executive coaching?
2. How emotionally aware are you? What areas need development?
3. How can one become more emotionally aware?

Chapter 11

Coachee Skill 6: Learning How To Dialogue

Introduction

Executive coaching is a conversation, a talk that centres on the professional learning and development of the coachee. Like all conversations, it can take on many forms:

1. A monologue where one person is speaking (eg., if the executive coach is giving a lecturette on how to manage a difficult person in the team).
2. A negotiation (where the coaching contract is being devised).
3. A discussion where a coach and coachee are working together on an intervention to work with an employee who is off with long term sickness.
4. A debate where there is usually a win/lose dimension (looking at the pros and cons of challenging a direct report). A debate can be an argument where one person is trying to convince the other about the rightness of their position (where an executive coach is trying to persuade the coachee not to resign at this stage).

While all these modes of conversation have their place in executive coaching and can be helpful methods of learning, we are suggesting that the best overall method of the coaching conversation is dialogue.

What Is Dialogue?

...Dialogue presents itself as an indispensable component of the process of both learning and knowing...

Executive coaching is a relational learning experience and dialogue is the conversation best suited to realize that learning: "I engage in dialogue because I recognize the social and not merely the individualistic character of knowing.... Dialogue presents itself as an indispensable component of the process of both learning and knowing (Freire and Macedo, 1995: 379). Because dialogue is "thinking together in relationship", when that relationship is one of trust, solidarity and empathy, then it becomes an exchange (a collective mindfulness) that can result in transformational learning. Senge, Kleiner, Roberts, Ross and Smith (1994) describe how dialogue can lead to "shared visions that live in our ongoing conversations about what we seek together to create" (p.24). It seems to us that the latter could be a wonderful definition of executive coaching: "A relationship of trust where, through the conversation called dialogue executive coaches and coachees create shared visions about how the coachee can live and work more effectively". Conversations change us for better or worse.

Here are some definitions of dialogue:

1. "Dialogue means a flow of meaning. It is a conversation in which we think together in relationship" (Isaac, 1999).
2. "Dialogue is the encounter of those addressed to the common task of learning and acting" (Freire, 1994:74).
3. "Dialogue is talk – a special kind of talk – that affirms the person-to-person relationship between discussants and which acknowledges their collective right and intellectual capacity to make sense of the world "(Dixon, 1998: 59).

Exercise

Look and select some conversation on TV and see if you can decide what kind of talk is taking place: is it a discussion, a monologue, a debate, an argument?

Features Of Dialogue

The features that distinguish dialogue from other forms
of conversation include the following:

*...dialogue is not
a difference in
technique but
a difference in
relationship...*

1. It is based on a certain kind of relationship. (Dixon (1998: 63) writes: "I am suggesting that dialogue is not a difference in technique but a difference in relationship". The relationship is one of valuing, respect, and equality. Dialogue is a meeting of people who come together to learn from each other.
2. It is a certain stance of humility towards learning. Knowing I do not know all there is to know allows me to come to others with openness to learning.
3. Dialogue acknowledges that we each see the world from a certain perspective (individual psychological truth) and that for each of us, there are other legitimate perspectives.
4. Dialogue does not have a preexisting outcome – those taking part are never certain where the conversation might go. Dialogue therefore means being open to various outcomes – the way forward.

Isaac (1999) outlines four features of dialogue:

1. The ability to listen (to myself, to others, to other perspectives).
2. The ability to respect (others, their views).
3. The ability to suspend (my own certainty, my own truth).
4. The ability to voice (to articulate, to say, to allow and help others to voice their thoughts and feelings).

We could see executive coaching as a form of "play". This is not to trivialize work or the people with whom one works, but to bring a curious and inquiring attitude to work that allows us to consider other ways of thinking about it. In a sense this is what dialogue does too. It plays with thoughts, ideas, stories, other perspectives, viewpoints, opinions, intuitions, hunches, theories, and frameworks as ways of approaching helpful actions. Generative learning or generative dialogues are terms used to show how talk leads to action.

Difficulties Of Dialogue

There are a number of blocks to dialogue. One of them is certainty (fundamentalism is the most extreme form of certainty) which does not allow participants to be open to other ways of knowing.

Creating the conditions for the kind of openness that leads to dialogue is not easy. It demands openness and "indifference" to where the outcome will lead. For those committed to an existing outcome or destination, dialogue can become impossible. Alvesson and Skoldberg (2000) capture this trap well:

If someone has dedicated almost all her career to a particular theory, then her repertoire will be restricted. Prestructured understandings dominate seeing. The capacity for reflection, if not altogether eliminated, is at least reduced. If one has worked a lot on a particular theory, one becomes, as a rule, emotionally attached to it. The empirical material will tend by and large to confirm the theory, (Alvesson and Skoldberg, 2000: 250).

This is where "downloading" becomes a substitute. We find and interpret information that sustains our existing stance. We change within the mould rather than allow ourselves to question the mould itself. Dialogue is a form of executive coaching conversation that opens the mind and the heart to other ways of thinking, seeing and doing. Not to be open makes it extremely difficult to dialogue.

Other conditions are equally important eg., the absence of shame and embarrassment. Both these affect learning dramatically and curtail the ability to be vulnerable and to "not know" or, at least to admit to myself or others that I do not know.

Multicultural Aspects Of The Executive Coaching Process

...Dealing with differences is a major challenge in coaching...

Conversations are between people and people differ in an amazing amount of ways. Those differences can all too easily become ways of dividing us or, in dialogue, hopefully become enrichments. Dealing with differences is a major challenge in coaching, not just differences between executive coach and coachee, but all the differences that emerge in the modern multicultural workplace.

We need to keep open our awareness of how issues of difference may impact on our work: issues of race, disability, age, gender, sexual orientation, religion, politics, language, culture and ethnicity. When we are working with a person from a different culture, we will need to take care to enquire into the 'norms' of that culture and take care not to assume that they are the same as ours. Generally, it is easy to enquire about the most obvious behavioural cues (dress, eating habits etc); less easy about more embedded beliefs and assumptions about life and work (those that we likely take for granted or value without thinking).

Some useful questions to ask of ourselves in your work contexts:

1. How may this person be seeing me?
2. What do I bring to this relationship in terms of my background that may subtly influence the relationship?
3. How aware am I of the impact of my behaviour, assumptions and attitudes on other people I have worked with? What can I learn from my experience of my impact on others?
4. How may the political context in which I am functioning influence the relationship?
5. What do I need to know about this person's race/culture/sexual orientation etc, in order to help him/her effectively or to have a good working relationship?
6. What reading can I do that will help me in understanding differences?
7. Can I imaginatively put myself into the 'shoes' of the other person and begin to get a sense of how he/she experiences his/her world?
8. What prejudices do I have that may hamper our relationship. Am I willing to be really honest with myself about these and work to address them?
9. If you are working in a culture that is not your own, what steps have you taken to get to know the norms and assumptions of your host culture?
10. What assumptions are you bringing from your culture of origin that would be viewed by others as eccentric at best, or pathological and dangerous at worst?

Conclusion

*...Coaching
is a form of
conversation
closer to dialogue
than to any other
form of talk...*

Coaching is a form of conversation closer to dialogue than to any other form of talk. In dialogue, both parties (executive coach and coachee) work together towards conclusions, resolutions and solutions. These do not necessarily preexist and in the openness and discussion and honesty of executive coaching, the best way forward emerges. Like so many other areas of executive coaching it is here, in the conversation we call coaching, that issues of power emerge – such issues have to be dealt with openly (through dialogue) so that power is used to empower rather than disempower.

Example

Emily talks about personal issues to her executive coach. She shares that her deep commitment and belief in Christianity makes it very difficult for her to be open to other religions, a number of which are espoused by employees in their work setting. Her values are quite traditional and she is having difficulties working with gay and lesbian staff. Things have come to a crisis because a member of her staff has asked her to arrange for a prayer room for Muslims in the work environment to facilitate their daily prayer regime.

Review And Discussion

1. What are the differences between monologue, negotiation, discussion, debate, argument and dialogue?
2. What are the characteristics of dialogue?
3. How do we set up the environment and relationships that allow dialogue to occur?
4. What difficulties do you see in your work situation that would make dialogue difficult to attain?

Chapter 12

Dealing With Problems In Executive Coaching

Introduction

While we hope that your experience of executive coaching and of being an executive coachee will be positive and contribute to your learning, we know there are times when problems in coaching make it a negative experience. Coaching is a co-operative endeavour and a relational learning process and it is important that you feel comfortable with your coach and the process of the sessions. Furthermore executive coaching is a triadic relationship between yourself, your executive coach and your organization. Frequently your own line manager will be involved in supporting you and evaluating the results of the executive coaching on your performance.

When the executive coaching alliance breaks down, it is often very difficult to repair and sometimes irreparable. We wish to outline some possible problems and suggest precautionary measures that you can take to deal with conflict should it arise. Conflict may arise from the following areas:

1. Your relationship with your executive coach. Conflicts here could be attributed to personality issues, to lack of compatibility around the coaching approach or with the contract. It could revolve around differences over assessments reports (written or verbal) or indeed over ethical and professional issues.
2. Issues around Contracts (two-way, three-way or four-way) – see Chapter 3 and Appendices 2, 3 and 4.
3. Your relationship with your organization. Conflicts with your organization could emerge from the coaching arrangement around administrative issues such as being given time off work to engage in coaching sessions; values in executive coaching being incompatible with the culture of the organization: disagreements around the agenda for coaching or assessment about how effective is executive coaching on changing and improving your performance.
4. Your relationship with your line-manager. Conflicts in this area can emerge from: not feeling supported enough by your line manager in mentoring you regarding the changes you are working on as a result of your executive coaching relationship; lack of agreement between you and your line manager on what ought to be the focus or agenda of coaching; misalignment of values between coaching and the values of your line manager, eg., in coaching, you learn to give more honest and direct feedback which is not a value appreciated by your line manager when you decide to give constructive feedback to him or her.

In this section we will look at some of the areas where conflict most commonly arises and then look at some strategies that can be set in place for dealing with conflict, should this arise.

Conflicts Related To Coaching Orientation

Differences in theoretical orientation can lead to difficulties and conflicts in executive coaching. All coaches will have training and experience in a certain approach or approaches to coaching, whether this is (to mention but a few): solution-focused; behavioural; cognitive-behavioural; integrative; existential; transactional analysis; neurolinguistic programming; hypnosis; transpersonal; psychodynamic. You may do well to ask your executive coach about his/her theoretical base and what that means in practice so that you have some basis for assessing if this suits you. In this regard, it is interesting to note that psychotherapy outcome research consistently suggests that there is no significant difference in outcome amongst different orientations (see Wampold, 2001) and it is highly likely that the same may apply to coaching despite the personal preferences of coaches. Some approaches are more directive, others more nondirective and facilitative of dialogue. As different frameworks are linked with particular styles of intervention, it would be good for you to have a conversation about the assumptions underpinning the approach used by your executive coach. By doing so you will know what to expect and can assess as you progress whether this suits you. What is good to know is that there are different models of coaching and if one particular approach does not work for you, you can seek out a coach with a different orientation to the work. Interesting points to note: Do you prefer a coach who is active in asking questions, giving you homework and guiding the work as you go along with the use of checklists? Or do you respond better to a coach who listens and facilitates you to find your own solutions through reflection and exploration of your thoughts and feelings about the situation? Or someone who does both?

Good questions to ask are:

1. What kind of interventions (ie., what does the executive coach do) are linked with this approach to the work?
2. What is the basic philosophy underpinning the approach?
3. What would a typical executive coaching session look like?
4. What will be expected of each of us over the course of coaching?

These questions would give you some idea of what to expect from the process of the sessions and from the coaching contract. You could then have an assessment period (eg., three sessions) in which you can judge whether this approach is working for you, and at the review make a decision about future sessions.

Conflicts Related To Style Of Coaching

...Some coaches have a formal style whilst others are far more informal and relaxed...

Coaching styles differ just as personalities do! Some coaches have a formal style whilst others are far more informal and relaxed in their approach. You may, for example, feel 'safer' with the person who is more formal and reveals little about themselves, whilst a more relaxed style may leave you feeling too uncertain and unfocused. Or formality and interpersonal distance may inhibit you and you will learn better with a more informal, personally communicative and exploratory approach. We know from research into personality styles that some people are more extroverted and outgoing whereas others are more introverted and internally reflective.

Generally learners prefer people (a) who allow exploration and experimentation and are not rule-bound; (b) who balance facilitating free discussion with input and suggestions while holding boundaries around the task; (c) who are warm and supportive and therefore approachable; and (d) who do not use coaching as a vehicle for doing therapy with the coachee but stick to the coaching task and focus (Carifio and Hess, 1987:245). If you feel the person is too distant from you, this may inhibit free communication; on the other hand, if the person is too relaxed and familiar, you may have an interesting chat but not have your coaching needs met. Ideally a balance between the two is usually best for learning. Experience suggests that the best coach is the person who shows respect, empathy, genuineness, concreteness and self-disclosure in his or her dealings with coachees whilst adhering closely to the contract and meeting the requests of the coachee.

The style of coaching can, of course, be negotiated and many coaches will be open to discussing what you want more or less of in the sessions. Your needs may also change over time and then the style of the sessions can optimally be renegotiated to suit your stage of development and your current challenges and learning needs.

Conflicts Related To Personality Issues

...It may happen that your coach misinterprets something you have said...

We sometimes hear of cases where there is a 'personality clash' between a coachee and a coach which can lead to a break or rupture in the working alliance. All of the above factors may be involved. Such ruptures are often the result of misunderstandings in communication and you would be well advised to raise such matters as soon as possible after they have arisen with a view to resolving the differences. It may happen that your coach misinterprets something you have said, or he/she may make a mistake about an appointment, such as getting the time wrong, or he/she may not have read something that you sent in advance. Such mistakes are part of most relationships and are best resolved by openly sharing feelings and clearing up any misperceptions. It is important to share your disappointments, feelings and expectations so that your executive coach can understand what is particularly important to you. Clear, open communication is at the heart of effective coaching.

You also need to be alert to the occasions when the rupture may be due to your own 'defensiveness'. For example, the coach may have given you feedback you experienced as hurtful or undermining even though the coach may have tried to couch the feedback in as specific and helpful a manner as possible. We all tend to be left with legacies from childhood in the form of beliefs about ourselves that may be unhelpful (eg., that I am stupid; or inadequate; or selfish; or too demanding; or 'too much' for other people). Something that the coach says may tap into your own negative belief system and you may go into a negative downward spiral without the coach even realising the unwitting impact of his/her statements. When you cannot sort this out by yourself, it may be best to bring the issue back to a coaching session and see if there is a 'grain of truth' in the criticism that has become all encompassing. What we are suggesting here is that both you and the coach can hold the responsibility for keeping the working alliance open and well-functioning as a learning space for you.

Conflicts Related To The Contract(s)

There may be conflicts that arise because of a lack of clarity about the nature of the contract. As Peltier (2001) points out, although there are many similarities in the ethics of coaching and of counselling/psychotherapy, there are also significant areas of difference. Significantly, he raises the issue of who is the client in the coaching? This question arises when there is a third-party payer, not in a private coaching arrangement that takes place outside of the workplace. When a company hires a coach to work with an executive and pays for the service, who is really the client? The executive? The company? Or both? Peltier asks: "To whom does the coach owe loyalty?" (2001: 226). Clearly the first loyalty of the coach is to the coachee but there is no simple answer to this problem if the company has hired the coach. Usually a company will expect that the coaching will relate to current business needs. This becomes an issue if the aims of the coaching begin to diverge from the company's goals. In a third-party contract of this kind, it is essential that clear contractual agreements are set in place at the start between the company representative, the coach and you as the coachee. Such a contract would cover how any 'reporting' is done and what elements of the coaching would be up for discussion. However, not all problems can be foreseen and sometimes you may need to request a review of the contract if your needs no longer match those of the company. An associated problem as Peltier (2001) also points out is that of the boundaries of confidentiality. These need to be clearly agreed and set out at the start. It is your right as a coachee to know what if any information will be passed back to the company and exactly what information would fall into that category. A clear pre-emptive contract at the outset will mean that you know where you stand and how the three-cornered contract will operate. It is also important to establish how this information will be relayed; it is usually best to set up an agreement that involves joint meetings so that you are present at any discussions about yourself and your work. In this way, you will be part of any discussions related to the coaching contract. If you are worried or anxious about any part of the various coaching contracts aAgreed, then ask for clarification and, if need be, for re-negotiation. It is important to get it right.

Conflicts With Your Company Or Organization

Not being given the support to ensure executive coaching is successful can create conflict. Many companies set up executive coaching without having thought through the implications of what it means in terms of time. It comes as a surprise to them to realize that they have not budgeted for time, even when they have made financial arrangements. It is worthwhile assessing for yourself the amount of time you will need to successfully engage in preparing for your executive coaching sessions, engaging in those sessions, evaluating afterwards and doing homework emerging from coaching. If conflict raises its head in this context then it's best to engage your own line manager to help you resolve it. His or her support will be invaluable here and will also ensure they are on your side vis a vis the effectiveness of the coaching arrangement.

…We have had instances of individuals who have left jobs as a result of executive coaching…

Our experience has taught us that organizations rarely think about the conflict in values that might emerge in setting up executive coaching for their staff. We have had instances of individuals who have left jobs as a result of executive coaching where they have faced up to the fact that their values (often only articulated in the coaching sessions) are not compatible with the values of the organization. eg. amount of time spent at work, work/ life imbalance and in one instance where the company involved made cigarettes.

A third area for potential conflict is in disagreement on the agenda for coaching. It needs to be crystal clear who sets that agenda. Some organizations are clear that they do and instruct both executive coach and coachee about the areas where they need to see changes. Where this is not clear, then two differing agendas can clash. The organization is expecting to see changes in performance A while the executive coach and coachee are working on performance B. This can also be an area of conflict between you and your direct line manager who has identified clear areas where he or she needs to see changes.

Assessment about the effectiveness of coaching on your performance can be a further fertile field for conflict. At the end of the day, however, the organization wants to see changes (that's what they are paying for). And the changes they want to see are external ie., in behaviour and performance. Coachees may feel that their coaching sessions are incredibly helpful in giving insights, ideas, theories, frameworks and models and even be an extremely valuable addition to their personal lives. But if there are not changes in work performance all these may be considered irrelevant to Human Resources or the line manager.

Conflict With Your Line-Manager

You may not feel supported enough by your line manager in mentoring you regarding the changes you are working on as a result of your executive coaching relationship. Many line-managers do not see it as their task to be involved directly or even indirectly in the coaching arrangement. They often see it as a "private" matter between executive coach and coachee and either do not want to interfere or feel they cannot. Either way, the coachee can feel a bit abandoned and not given enough encouragement or direct support in implementing the changes emerging from coaching. Some kind of agreement or contract between you and your line manager which outlines roles and responsibilities for each of you (expectations too) will not only help clarify these but give you a foundation on which to review them.

...in coaching, you may learn to give more honest and direct feedback which may not be a value appreciated by your line manager...

Misalignment of values between coaching and the values of your line manager can also arise eg., in coaching, you may learn to give more honest and direct feedback which may not be a value appreciated by your line manager when you decide to give constructive feedback to him or her.

Critical Moments In Executive Coaching

We do not want to end this section without dealing with the fact that all relationships hit crisis moments where ruptures and interruptions in the relationships raise their heads. These critical moments in the relationship are not necessarily signs that the relationship is heading for the rocks: at times, they can be quite the opposite and are indicators that something needs review or that the relationship is being challenged to reach a new level and deal with a new factor. However, executive coaches and coachees sometimes panic when their relationship seems to hit an impasse or be blocked. In a fascinating piece of research De Haan and his colleagues at Ashridge Centre for Coaching interviewed a number of executive coaches about critical moments in their coaching work (2007). What they discovered was that critical moments in coaching are:

1. Unforeseen.
2. Bring heightened emotions.
3. Give rise to tensions within the relationship.

These in turn give rise to anxiety and sometimes doubt on the part of the coach, which in turn result in potential opportunities for insight and change in the relationship or lead to a breakdown. It can be a "make or break" situation. De Haan et al. (2007) isolated characteristics of these critical relationship moments:

1. Heightened emotion for the coachee.
2. Heightened emotion for the coach eg., feelings of anger, fear, sadness, doubts, inadequacy.
3. A tension or tension in the relationship (a cross roads).

They outline steps/stages in the process involved in the emergence of critical moments in coaching:

1. All moments start with action or raw emotion.
2. Counteractions – often a defensive reaction: an immediate, unprocessed response.

3. Interior dialogue (or internal ethical dilemma). This is thinking-after-the-event. A distancing.
4. Explicit distancing in the relationship (not turning up).
5. Shared reflection – explore the state of their own relationship.
6. Deepening of the relationship (sometimes re-contracting).
7. Satisfactory change for the coachee (often new insight).
8. Breakdown of the relationship.
9. Unknown future.

What the researchers found made the difference between whether or not the coaching relationship continues depends on the kind of interventions used by the executive coach. These included:

1. Confronting or challenging the coachee with interest and acceptance.
2. Providing feedback to the coachee in the here and now about what was happening.
3. Sharing their own feelings with the coachee.
4. Reflecting on the possible link to the coachee's issues and feelings.
5. Helping the coachee to clarify their thinking.
6. Providing direction.

...we want you to be alert to the signs that your coaching relationship might be at an end...

Coaches and coachees do not back away from these moments of rupture – they stay with them and make them into "generative moments" in their coaching relationship. We mention their research to encourage you to stay with awkward, difficult or challenging moments in coaching in order to see if these moments are asking both you and your coach to deepen the relationship and face new challenges. On the other hand, we want you to be alert to the signs that your coaching relationship might be at an end or that it would be unhelpful for you to continue it. Knowing the difference is quite a skill.

Setting In Place Strategies For Dealing With Conflict

When setting up a coaching contract, it is worthwhile setting in place strategies for dealing with any potential conflict. These may include the following steps, some preventative, and some palliative:

1. At the outset express your expectations of coaching very clearly and request the same of the coach so that you are both clear about what is expected on both sides.
2. Sometimes it is good to start by approaching conflicts as opportunities for learning and not necessarily as breakdowns in relationships. When we ask: "What is this conflict really about and what role am I playing in it?" we can often find conflict a great source of learning.
3. Make a contract that focuses on your learning goals for the duration of the initial contract (usually these are made for four to six sessions) and also come to each coaching session with a clear focus on what you wish to gain from the session.
4. Suggest a mutual agreement to give regular ongoing feedback to one another about the process of the coaching.
5. Agree to a regular review at the end of each session to refer back to the overall goals of the coaching.
6. Make an agreement with yourself to raise any area of conflict when it arises (or as soon as possible after the event) and not to let it fester and get worse over time!

7. If there is conflict, try to sort this out directly with your coach. You would be well advised to set out clearly in advance the points you wish to discuss so that you are both clear about the agenda for the meeting. That way you will be able to focus on the central conflict area(s).

8. If it proves impossible for you and your coach to resolve the matter or the rupture seems to be widening, we suggest that you approach a third person to act as mediator. This would generally be someone from outside your immediate work situation but a person you both feel you could trust and with whom you could both work. At best, this process could lead to a resolution and clarity about how you move forward; or, at worst, it may facilitate a parting between the two of you without rancour and resentment. Ending well is a good outcome too.

It is good to realize that sometimes certain relationships do not work and that is that.

Your executive coach will probably belong to a professional organization, subscribe to a code of ethics and have indemnity insurance for his or her coaching work. If you felt you executive coach was or has been unethical or seriously unprofessional, then it is possible to make a complaint or take out an ethical charge against him or her. Such an action would not be taken lightly but it does remain another possible way of dealing with conflict areas in executive coaching. Your executive coach will be able to provide you with a copy of the Code of Ethics (or the Ethical Framework) to which he/she subscribes and the Professional Body of which he/she is a member.

Conclusion

...we hope that through talking about the differences that these differences can become sources of learning...

While we have looked at some conflicts that may arise within coaching we have, by no means, listed all possible difficulties. It is worthwhile being prepared for when relationships go wrong, for whatever reason. Overall, we hope that through talking about the differences that these differences can become sources of learning. If need be, having others involved to help us resolve difficulties is simply an acknowledgement that there are times when we need referees and observers who have an "outside" stance regarding our "inside" way of seeing what is taking place.

Example

You have reason to believe that your Executive Coach, Roger, has been contacted by HR. You know that your name has been forwarded for Head of Department and you suspect that the HR Director is interested in getting Roger's opinion on your suitability (especially since Roger knows the industry in which you work very well). Roger has mentioned nothing to you about any contact with HR. You picked up a hint from the HR Director. You are not sure what to do since nothing in your contract with Roger or with your organization allows for this informal contact.

Review And Discussion

1. What do you think is the best way of dealing with conflicts in relationships? Can you think of an example from your own personal or work environment where you have had to resolve a difference or difficulty? What would you do differently now?

2. What makes conflict in relationships (and in particular in the executive coaching relationship) a difficult process?
3. What makes dealing with conflict a difficult process in itself?

References And Further Reading

Alvesson, M. and Skoldberg, K. (2000) Reflexive Methodology: New Vistas for Qualitative Research. London: Sage.

Bachkirova, T. and Cox, E (2005) A Bridge over Troubled Waters: Bring together Coaching and Counselling. Counselling at Work, 48, 2-9.

Belenky, M. et al. (1986) Women's Ways of Knowing: The Development of Self, Voice and Mind. New York: Basic Books.

Bluckert, P. (2006) Psychological Dimensions of Executive Coaching. Maidenhead: Open University Press.

Bolton, G. (2001) Reflective Practice. London: Paul Chapman.

Bond, M and Holland, S. (1998) Skills of Clinical Supervision for Nurses. Buckingham: Open University Press.

Boud, D., Keogh, R. and Walker, D (eds) (1985) Reflection: Turning Experience into Learning. London: Kogan Page.

Brockbank, A. and McGill, I. (1998) Facilitating Reflective Learning in Higher Education. Buckingham: Open University Press.

Campbell, J.M. (2000) Becoming an Effective Supervisor: A workbook for Counselors and Psychotherapists. Philadelphia: Taylor and Francis.

Carifio, M and Hess, A. (1987) Who is the Ideal Supervisor. Professional Psychology, 18, 3, 244-250.

Carroll, M. (2004) The Psychological Contract in Organizations. In, R. Tribe and M. Morrissey (eds) Professional and Ethical Issues for Psychologists, Psychotherapists and Counsellors. London: Brunner-Routledge.

Carroll, M. (1996) Counselling Supervision: Theory, Skills and Practice. London: Cassell.

Casement, P. (1985) On Learning from the Patient. London: Tavistock.

CIPD (2004, 2005, 2006) Training and development Survey Reports. London: CIPD.

Chartered Institute of Personnel and Development. (2004) Coaching and Buying Coaching – A Guide. London: CIPD.

Clarkson, P. and Gilbert, M. (1991) Training Counsellor Trainers and Supervisor. IN W. Dryden and B. Thorne (eds) Training and Supervision for Counsellors in Action. London: Sage.

Claxton, G. (1999) Wise Up: The Challenge of Lifelong Learning. London: Bloomsbury.

Clutterbuck, D. (2007) Coaching the Team at Work. London: Nicholas Brealey.

Clutterbuck, D and Megginson, D. 2005) Making Coaching
Work: Creating a Coaching Culture. London: CIPD.

Connor, M. and Pokora, J. (2007) Coaching and Mentoring at Work: Developing
Effective Practice. Maidenhead, Berkshire: Open University Press.

Day, A., De Haan, E., Blass, E., Sills, C. and Bertie, C. (2007) Critical Moments in the
Coaching Relationship: Does Supervision Help (Draft Article for Journal Submission).

Dewey, J. (1933) How we Think. London: Heath.

Dickson, A. (2004) Difficult Conversations: What to say in
tricky situations without ruining your Relationship.

Dixon, N. (1998) Dialogue at Work. London: Lemos and Crane.

Downey, M (1999) Effective Coaching. London: Orion Business Books.

Driscoll, M.P. (2005) Psychology of Learning for Instruction.
International Edition: New York: Pearson

Flaherty, J (1999) Coaching: Evoking Excellence in
others. Woburn: MA: Butterworth-Heinemann.

Freire, P. (1998) Teachers as Cultural Workers. Oxford: Westview Press.

Freire, P and Macedo, D.P. (1995) A dialogue: Culture, language
and Race. Harvard Educational Review, 65 (3), 377-403.

Gallwey, T. The Inner Game of Tennis. London: Texere Publishing.

Gardner, H. (1999) Intelligence Reframed. New York: Basic Books.

Gilbert, M. and Evans, K. (2000) Psychotherapy Supervision: An Integrative Relational
Approach to Psychotherapy Supervision. Buckingham: Open University Press.

Gilbert, M. and Sills, C. (1999) Training for Supervision Evaluation. In E. Holloway
and M. Carroll (eds) Training Counselling Supervisors. London: Sage.

Goleman, D. (1996) Emotional Intelligence. London: Blooomsbury.

Goleman, D. (1998) Working with Emotional Intelligence. London: Bloomsbury.

Grace-Roland, M. (2008) Dimensions of Mentoring Relationships:
A Holistic Perspective. PhD, Antioch University.

Grant, A. M. (2006) An integrated Goal-focused approach to
executive coaching. In D.R. Stober and A.M. Grant (Eds.) Evidence
Based Coaching Handbook. New Jersey: Wiley and Sons.

Grant, A. and Greene, J. (2001) It's your life – what are you
going to do with it: coach yourself. London; Pearson.

Grief, S. (2007) Advances in research in Coach Outcomes, International Coaching Psychology Review, 2, 3, 222-245.

Hawkins, P. and Smith, N. (2006) Coaches, Mentors and Organizational consultants: Supervision and Development. Milton Keynes: Open University Press.

Hawkins, P. and Shohet, R. (1989) Supervision in the Helping Professions. Milton Keynes: Open University Press (2nd Edition, 2000).

Hewson, J. (1999) Training supervisors to contract in supervision. In E. Holloway and M. Carroll (eds) Training Counselling Supervisors. London: Sage.

Holloway and M. Carroll (eds) Training Counselling Supervisors. London: Sage.

Honey, P. and Mumford, A. (1992) The Manual of Learning Styles. Maidenhead: Peter Honey.

Inskipp, F. (1999) Training Supervisees to use Supervision. In, E. Holloway and M. Carroll (eds) Training Counselling Supervisors: Strategies, Methods and Techniques. London: Sage.

Inskipp, F. & Proctor, B. (1993) Making the Most of Supervision Part 1. Middlesex: Cascade Publications. (2nd Edition, 2001).

Inskipp, F. & Proctor, B. (1995) Making the Most of Supervision. Part 2. Middlesex: Cascade Publications. (2nd Edition, 2001).

Isaac, W. (1999) Dialogue and the Art of Communication. New York: Doubleday.

Jarvis, J. (2004) Coaching and Buying Coaching Services. London: CIPD.

Jarvis, J., Lane, D. and Fillery-Travis, A. (2006) The Case for Coaching: Making Evidence Based Decisions on Coaching. London: CIPD.

Kaberry, S. (1995) Abuse in Supervision. M.Ed. Dissertation. University of Birmingham.

Kahler, T. and Capers, H. (1974) The Miniscript. Transactional Analysis Journal, 1, 26-42.

Kahler, T. (1978) Transactional Analysis Revisited. Little Rock: Human Development Publications.

Kaufman, G. (1992) Shame: The Power of Crying. Rochester: Scherknew Books.

Kegan, R. (1994) In Over our Heads: The Mental Demands of Modern Life. San Francesco: Jossey-Bass.

Kets de Vries, M. (2007) The Leader on the Couch. San Francesco: Jossey-Bass.

Kilburg, R (1996) Towards a conceptual understanding and definition of executive coaching, Consulting Psychology Journal, 49 (4), 281-99.

Kline, N. (1999) Time to Think: Listening to Ignite the Human Mind. London: Ward Lock.

Knapmann and Morrison, T. (1998) Making the Most of Supervision. Pavilion.

Kolb, D. (1984) Experiential Learning. Englewood Cliffs, NJ: Prentice Hall.

Lammers, W. (1999) Training in Group and Team Supervision. In E. Holloway and M.Carroll (eds) Training Counselling Supervisors. London: Sage.

Law, H., Ireland, J. and Hussain, Z. (2007) The Psychology of Coaching, Mentoring and Learning. Chicester: Wiley.

Mayer, J. and Salovey, P. (1997) What is emotional intelligence? In, P. Salovey and S. Shulter (eds) Emotional Intelligence and Emotional Development. New York: Basic Books.

Mezirow, J. and Associates (2000) Learning as Transformational: Critical Perspectives on a Theory of Progress. San Francisco: Jossey-Bass.

Moloney, K. (2005) The Frog Prince: Giving Tips on How to Choose a Coach. Coaching at Work, November.

Moskowitz, S.A., and Rupert, P.A. (1983) Conflict Resolution within the Supervisory Relationship. Professional Psychology: Research and Practice, 14, 632 - 641.

Newfeldt. S. (1999) Training in Reflective Processes in Supervision. In E. Holloway and M. Carroll (eds) Training Counselling Supervisors. London: Sage.

O'Broin, A. and Palmer, S. (2007) Reappraising the coach-client relationship: the unassuming change-agent in coaching. In Palmer, S. and Whybrow, A. (Eds) Handbook of Coaching Psychology. London: Routledge.

Ofman, D. (2001) Core Qualities: A gateway to Human Resources. Schiedam, the Netherlands: Scriptum.

Orme, G. (2991) Emotionally Intelligent Living. Glasgow: Crown House Publishers.

Ostell, A., Beverstock, S. and Wright, P. (1999) Interpersonal Skills of Managing Emotions at Work. The Psychologist, 12, 1, 30 - 34.

Palmer, S. and Whybrow, A. (2007) Handbook of Coaching Psychology. Hove, East Sussex: Routledge.

Parsloe, E. and Wray, M. (2000) Coaching and Mentoring: Practical Methods to improve Learning. London: Kogan Page.

Passmore, J and Gibbes, C. (2007) The State of Executive Coaching Research: What does the current literature tell us and what's next for coaching research? International Coaching Psychology Review, 2, 2, 116 - 127.

Peltier, B. (2001) The Psychology of Executive Coaching. New York: Brunner- Routledge.

Proctor, B. (2000) Group Supervision: A Guide to Creative Practice. London: Sage.

Robinson, W. L. (1974) Conscious Competence: the Mark of the Competent Instructor. Personnel Journal, 53, 538 - 539.

Rock, D. (2006) Quiet Leadership: Six Steps to Transforming Performance at Work. New York: Collins.

Schon, D. (1983) The Reflective Practitioner. New York: Basic Books.

Schon, D. (1987) Educating the Reflective Practitioner. San Francesco: Jossey-Bass.

Scott, S. (2002) Fierce Conversation: Achieving success at work and in life: One conversation at a time. London: Piatkus.

Senge, P., Kleiner, A., Ross, R., Roberts, C. and Smith, B. (1994) The fifth discipline field book: Strategies and Tools for Building a Learning Organization. London: Nicholas Brealey.

Sperry, L. (2004) Executive Coaching: the Essential Guide for Mental Health Professionals. New York: Brunner-Routledge.

Stokes, P. (2007) Two can play that Game, Coaching at Work, 2, 6, 58.

Stone, D, Patton, B., and Heen, S (2000) Difficult Conversation: How to Discuss what matters Most. London: Penguin.

Scharmer, C. O. (2007) Theory U: Leading from the Future as it Emerges. Cambridge, Mass: SOL Publications.

Stolterberg, C.D., McNeill, B.W. and Delworth, U. (1998) IDM Supervision: An Integrated Development Model for Supervising Therapists and Counselors. San Francisco: Jossey-Bass.

The Executive Coaching Handbook (Principles and Guidelines for a Successful Coaching Partnership. (2004) at: HYPERLINK "http://www.executivecoachingforum.com" www.executivecoachingforum.com.

Vaill, P. (1996) Learning as a Way of Being. San Francesco: Jossey-Bass.

Wampold, B. (2001) The Great Psychotherapy Debate. New Jersey: Lawrence Erlbaum Associates.

Weisinger, H. (1998) Emotional Intelligence at Work. San Francesco: Jossey-Bass.

Whybrow, A. and Henderson, V. (2007) Concepts to support the integration and sustainability of coaching initiatives within organizations. In Palmer, S. and Whybrow, A. (Eds) Handbook of Coaching Psychology. London: Routledge.

Whyte (1994) The Heart Aroused. London: The Industrial Society.

Williams, P and Davis, D. (2002) Therapist as Life Coach: Transforming your Practice. New York: Norton.

Witherspoon, R. (2000) Staying Smart: Clarifying Goals and Roles. In. M. Goldsmith, L. Lyons and A. Freas (eds) Coaching for Leadership. San Francisco: Jossey-Bass.

Zachary, L (2000) The Mentor's Guide: Facilitating Effective Learning Relationships. San Francisco: Jossey-Bass.

Zohar, D. and Marshall, I. (2001) Spiritual Intelligence – The Ultimate Intelligence. London: Bloomsbury.

Appendix 1

Some Further Definitions Of Coaching And Executive Coaching

"Coaching is the art of facilitating the development, learning and performance of another" (School of Coaching).

"In the same way that athletic coaches help their teams or individuals to achieve excellent performances, workplace coaches need to help their teams and individual team members to reach their potential and deliver a personal best".

"Life coaching is a powerful human relationship where trained coaches assist people to design their future rather than get over their past... coaches aid clients in creating visions and goals for all aspects of their lives and creating multiple strategies to support achieving those goals " (Williams and Davis, 2002, xv).

Coaching is a dialogue between coach and client where they work together to define the issues and jointly construct a solution" (Green and Grant, 2003: 28).

"The aim (of mentoring and coaching) is to help and support people to manage their own learning in order that they may maximize their potential, develop their skills, improve their performance and enable them to become the person they want to be" (Parsloe and Wray, 220:22).

"Coaching is giving people a chance to examine what they are doing in the light of their intentions ... a coach is someone who builds a respectful relationship with a client and then researches the situations the client finds himself in, with particular emphasis on the client's interpretation of the events" (Flaherty, 1999).

"Professional Coaching is an ongoing partnership that helps clients produce fulfilling results in their personal and professional lives. Through the process of coaching, clients improve their performance and enhance the quality of their lives. In each meeting, the client chooses the focus of conversation, while the coach listens and contributes observations and questions. The interaction creates clarity and moves the client into action. Coaching accelerates the client's programme by providing greater focus and awareness of choice. Coaching concentrates on where clients are today and what they are willing to-do to get where they want to be tomorrow" (ICF Philosophy).

"A collaborative, individualized, solution-focused, results-oriented, systemic and stretching process in which the coach facilitates the enhancement of work performance, life experience, self directed learning and personal growth of the coachee. It should be evidence-based and incorporate ethical professional practice" (Grant 2000, 2006).

The art of facilitating the performance, learning and development of another" (Downey, 1999).

Appendix 2

Example Of A Two-Way Executive Coaching Contract

Executive Coaching Contract

This is an executive coaching contract between ....

and .... from ....

until its review (or ending) in ....

What Is Executive Coaching?

We are agreed that executive coaching is a contracted learning relationship personalized for individual executives (managers, leaders etc). It is a triadic relationship working in partnership with an executive coach (name), individual executive (name) and Company/ Organization/Manager (name). Its purpose is to develop (executive's name) skills, competencies, capabilities and potential in the light of short and long term company goals.

Practicalities:

We will meet for .... hours every .... at a time to be arranged at the end of each coaching session. We have agreed that each of us will ensure that there are no unnecessary interruptions (mobiles, phone, and people).

Procedures:

We have agreed that the following arrangements will take place in the following situations:

Cancellation of session

....

Non-attendance at coaching session

....

Where there are disagreements, disputes, conflict areas
between executive coach and client (coachee)

....

If there is need for extra coaching sessions

....

126

Contracts with others eg., an organization

For appeals

....

Keeping of notes

....

You are free to phone me if there is an emergency on the following number

....

What will you (coachee) do if I (the coach) am not available?

....

Guidelines:

The following guidelines/ground rules will guide our time together:

1. Confidentiality (what we mean by confidentiality is…).
2. Openness/honesty (about work done, the relationship, reports etc).
3. Line management issues that may pertain (especially if the coach is also the line-manager).
4. Gossip (any leakage of information in the systems).
5. Using feedback to learn.

Roles And Responsibilities:

We have agreed that, as executive coach, I will take responsibility for:

1. Time keeping.
2. Managing the overall agenda of sessions.
3. Giving feedback.
4. Monitoring the coaching relationship.
5. Creating a safe place/space.
6. Monitoring ethical and professional issues.
7. Keeping notes of sessions.
8. Drawing up the final reports (if needed).

We have agreed that, as coachee, you will responsible for:

1. Preparing for the coaching session.
2. Presenting in coaching.
3. Articulating your learning (objectives).
4. Applying learning from coaching (at work).
5. Feedback to self and to me.
6. Keeping notes of sessions.

Evaluation And Review:

We have agreed that informal evaluation of:

Client: ....

Coach: ....

Coaching: ....

Will take place every sixth session. Formal Evaluations will take place every year or as requested by either of us.

Re-Negotiation Of Contract:

At any time either party (coach and/or client) can initiate discussion around re-negotiation of the contract or any part of it. This will be done in advance so that there is preparatory time available.

Signed: .... (Coach) Date

Signed: .... (Client/s) Date

Example Of An Executive Coaching Contract (2)

Terms Of Business For Coaching, Counselling And Mentoring

Programme

We believe that as each person is an individual with individual issues and needs, each programme will require individual design. Programmes therefore might range from a limited series of sessions (typically 3 –6) focussed on very specific issues to broader development. In these latter cases, a typical programme might be 10 –15 sessions over 12 –18 months. A typical session will last 2-3 hours.

Conditions

It is a condition of any assignment that:

1. The individual is committed to the process and there is a belief that there exists the capability and desire to change.
2. There is an agreed brief between the individual, the consultant and the contracting party about the programme, the period and the desired outcomes.
3. All conversations between the individual and the consultant are confidential and will only be disclosed with the permission of the individual concerned.
4. This consultancy will not be held responsible for the subsequent work and lifestyle decisions that the individual may make.
5. This consultancy may refer the individual to any other competent body. Where additional cost is involved then this will only be enacted when suitable approval is given.
6. Once the programme is agreed, half the programme fee is immediately payable. The other half is payable at the end.
7. Sessions can be held anywhere, but will normally be in London or at …… Where the consultant is required to travel to meet the individual, travel time will be charged at half the hourly rate.
8. Appointments that are cancelled within 5 working days will be charged at the standard rate.
9. Direct expenses where applicable (travel, accommodation, materials etc.) will be charged at cost.
10. All fees are subject to VAT and payment is expected within 30 days.

Codes of Practice and Ethics

We adhere to the professional codes of the Chartered Institute of Personnel and Development, The British Association of Counselling and the British Psychological Society.

General

All recommendations made in any form are made in good faith and on the information available at the time. No statement in any proposal is deemed to be in any circumstance a representation, undertaking, warranty or contractual condition. We shall not be liable to the client for any losses, which are not reasonably foreseeable on acceptance of the proposal, or for any indirect or consequential losses, including loss of revenue, anticipated profits and claims by third parties.

(Our thanks to Jim Cannon for sharing this contract with us for his permission to reproduce it here)

An Executive Coaching Contract (3)

To: Name
Address,
City etc

Dear Name,

Executive Coaching Programme

Following our recent discussions, I am writing to outline my approach to working together incorporating the initial areas, which we discussed.

Purpose

The purpose of the programme is to facilitate your personal development thus ensuring your effectiveness in your role and, consequently, your contribution to the success of (the company name). My purpose in working with you is to enhance your performance and to support you in your aim for excellence.

Methodology

As we have already agreed, there are certain areas (shown below) that will form the starting point of our work together. As we discussed, these may change or be added to as we progress as a result of your own insights and input from others as we agree that may be helpful.

1. Managing upwards in the organization
2. Your boss and how to manage that relationship
3. Other key players and Sponsors – character of those relationships
4. Styles – yours and others
5. Communication type and frequency
6. Managing sideways
7. Who are your peers and what are the dynamics of those relationships?
8. Which do you need to work on?
9. Leading your team
10. Your leadership signature – values and priorities
11. Communicating your vision
12. Understanding and motivating direct reports
13. Communications processes 1 on 1 and team
14. Your style
15. Your self-confidence
16. How you prioritize and use my time
17. Developing relationships with senior level clients

The actual coaching process will be a combination of the following approaches:

1. Challenge and confrontation.

This relates to the ways you think, act and interact. Some of this process will be at a cognitive level in challenging your beliefs and understanding of people and their behaviour as well as your own. Some will be at an interpersonal level regarding the way that we interact in the programme together. There will be "on-line" feedback and discussion regarding your style and how that impacts.

2. Inputs

These are semi-formal conversations led by me on various topics. They will often be supported by handouts of various types or by your own note taking. It is very helpful if you keep a formal log of our sessions and take notes as we progress.

3. Tasking

You will be asked to try new ways of doing things and of thinking, and these will be followed up when you bring examples for discussion to the next session. Sometimes these will be formal, specified tasks, and sometimes they will consist of less precise and more challenging opportunities for the development of certain skills or insights.

4. Reading

There will be required reading and books will be recommended for you to purchase relating to specific topics. These are to be read, inwardly digested and to be reported on at the next session with practical examples of how the work has impacted on you in your work and personal life.

5. Iteration

Many of the topics to be covered interlink at various levels and therefore topics will often be re-visited in the context of the material under review. Some sessions may have to be repeated or approached from another angle.

6. Reviews

It is important to review, and this will be done regularly to help you judge your own progress and what you are gaining from the programme. We will want to involve (your boss's name) roughly half-way through the programme and then at the end to review progress and determine what further work may be needed. When such meetings take place, you will manage this interface which is intended to keep him/her informed of progress and to get input from him/her on his/her observations.

Typical Structure Of A Session:

Each session stands alone but is linked, particularly to the previous session, because of follow-up, and to the next session, because of reading and/or tasking. They are also all interlinked because the various topics to be covered are all facets of the interpersonal aspects of the programme. Each session is planned to be of one and a half hours, but the time may vary according to the topic in hand and the material brought for discussion.

Typically a session will consist of four parts, not necessarily of equal length:

1. Review of the previous session and tasking/reading.

2. Work-based material brought by you on interactions and style matters, for discussion.
3. Inputs by me on a given topic.
4. Tasking/ reading on the topic for review at the next session.

Programme Periodicity, Duration And Location Of Meetings

The programme, including any initial meeting with your manager, will take place over a maximum period of six months, a total of 15 hours during that period. The cost of this will be .... payable at the outset. One preengagement briefing meeting is included in this cost. Any other briefing meetings are chargeable at the rate of ..... per hour.

Sessions are arranged in advance, normally at two/three weekly intervals. This allows time for reading and tasking to be done and for practical, live, work-based material to be identified and brought to the following session. Meetings between the individual and the consultant are held at our own offices or at your premises in a private room as agreed at the outset. Unless for exceptional reasons, and agreed by us, the programme will be considered to be complete at the end of the 6 months from the date of the first one-to-one meeting. Planned meetings which are cancelled with 3 working days notice or less will be considered as used against the total hours planned.

Framework And Confidentiality

It is my experience that the greatest development can take place when this work is carried out within the bounds of strict confidentiality. We will not, therefore, without your permission, give to the company any content information arising during the programme. You are, of course, at liberty to discuss any aspect of the programme with whomsoever you wish, but we urge caution and prudence regarding this. The only exception would be:

If you are at risk of harming yourself or another person or are taking actions which are damaging to your employing organization.

In the unlikely event that your coach believes that the process is not delivering the changes and outputs required, your coach may, with prior notice to you, bring this to the attention of your manager and/or HR professional for three-way discussion.

Code Of Ethics And Complaints Procedure

Our coaching work is governed by the Ethical Guidelines of APECS (The Association for Professional Executive Coaching & Supervision).

Role Of Others

(Your boss – name) plays a key role in this coaching process. He/she is expected to give you specific feedback on the behavioural areas we agree to focus on. He/she will also be aware through his/her network of the ways in which your style is impacting others. At our review meetings he/she will get your input as to the progress you are making within the coaching programme and will feedback his/her observations to you.

Requirements For Success

To achieve success, you need to commit to:

1. Openness to the learning process.
2. Keeping thorough notes as a learning log for reference.
3. Diligence in carrying out the tasks and reading prescribed.
4. Frequent and proper practice of new approaches, skills and techniques.
5. Attendance at the sessions we have arranged.
6. Bringing proper and appropriate material for discussion and work.
7. A sense of discretion in not discussing the programme and its tasks in unsuitable ways or with anyone who might seek to undermine its efficacy.

I am looking forward to our continuing work together.

Yours sincerely,

Our Thanks to John O'Brien for sharing this contract with us and giving us permission to reproduce it here)

Appendix 5

Executive Coachee Data Form

Name:

....

Home Addres:

....

Business Address:

....

Phone numbers

....

Fax numbers

....

Email address

....

Where best to contact you/leave messages

....

Preferred means of communication

....

Occupation/Job (explain a bit)

....

....

Preferred coaching schedule (telephone, face to face etc)

....

Family (present)

....

Family (of origin)

....

What do you want from Coaching? Do you have specific goals?

....

....

....

What do you want to focus on first of all?

....

....

....

How do you learn best?

....

....

How can I facilitate your learning?

....

....

How would I block your learning?

....

....

Any other information that would help me in coaching you?

....

....

....

Appendix 6

Executive Coaching Session Evaluation Form (For Coachee)

What went particularly well in our coaching session?

What relationship challenges did we face?

Were we communicating effectively with each other?

Were we candid and open in our communication?

What did we not talk about (avoided)?

What learning challenges emerged?

Any external factors that impacted on our session?

What three actions could improve the quality of our coaching arrangement:

Date:

Appendix 7

An Evaluation Feedback Form For Coachees (To Their Coaches)

Am I (your executive coach) providing sufficient support to facilitate your learning?

....

....

Have we identified sufficient and varied opportunities for your learning?

....

....

Is the coaching relationship productive? Anything we need to discuss?

....

....

....

Is the feedback I give thoughtful, candid and constructive?

....

....

Is there a good balance of support and challenge in our coaching?

....

....

Are there areas we do not talk about that should be the focus of a conversation?

....

....

Are the topics of discussion in our coaching making an
impact on your performance in life or work?

....

....

What seems to you to be the next challenge in your development?

....

....

What is most helpful about our coaching arrangement? What is least helpful?

....

....

Is there anything you would like me to stop doing? Start doing? Increase? Decrease?

....

....

How can we be more accountable in our coaching arrangement to others?
To your staff? To relevant organizations? To our Profession?

....

....

....

Date: ....

Descriptions Of The Four Learning Styles

Activists

Activists like to take direct action. They are enthusiastic and welcome new challenges and experiences. They are primarily interested in the here and now. They are less interested in what has happened in the past or in putting things into a broader context. They like to have a go, try things out and participate. They like to be the centre of attention. So, in summary, Activists like:

1. To think on their feet
2. To have short sessions
3. Plenty of variety
4. The opportunity to initiate
5. To participate and have fun

Reflectors

Reflectors like to think about things in detail before taking action. They take a thoughtful approach. They are good listeners and prefer to adopt a low profile. They are prepared to read and re-read and will welcome the opportunity to repeat a piece of learning. So, in summary, Reflectors like:

1. To think before acting
2. Thorough preparation
3. To research and evaluate
4. To make decisions in their own time
5. To listen and observe

Theorists

Theorists like to see how things fit into an overall pattern. They are logical and objective systems people who prefer a sequential approach to problems. They are analytical, pay great attention to detail and tend to be perfectionists. So, in summary, Theorists like:

1. Concepts and models
2. To see the overall picture
3. To feel intellectually stretched
4. Structure and clear objectives
5. Logical presentation of ideas.

Pragmatists

Pragmatics like to see how things work in practice. They enjoy experimenting with new ideas. They are practical, down to earth and like to solve problems. They appreciate the opportunity to try out what they have learned/are learning. So, in summary, Pragmatists like:

1. To see the relevance to their work
2. To gain practical advantage from learning
3. Credible role models
4. Proven techniques
5. Activities to be real

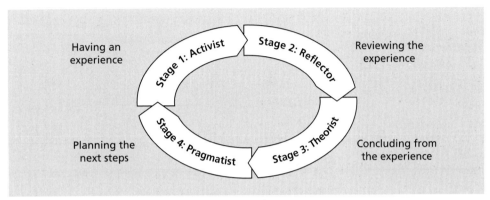

The Learning Styles Diagram

Thanks to Peter Honey Publications for permission to include the above descriptions of the Learning Styles. Access to the Learning Styles Inventory can be found at www.peterhoney.com.

Questionnaire On Multiple Intelligences

Please complete the following questionnaire by assigning a numerical value to each of the statements which you consider represent you. If you agree that the statement very strongly represents you assign a 5. If the statement does not represent you assign a 0. Use the numbers 5 – 1 to grade each statement

1. I am skillful in working with objects ....
2. I have a good sense of direction ....
3. I have a natural ability to sort out arguments between friends ....
4. I can remember the words to music easily ....
5. I am able to explain topics which are difficult and make them clear ....
6. I always do things one step at a time ....
7. I understand myself well and understand why I behave as I do ....
8. I enjoy community activities and social events ....
9. I learn well from talks, lectures and listening to others ....
10. When listening to music I experience changes in mood ....
11. I enjoy puzzles, crosswords, logical problems ....
12. Charts, diagrams, visual displays are important for my learning ....
13. I am sensitive to the moods and feelings of those around me ....
14. I learn best when I have to get up and do it for myself ....
15. I need to see something in front of me before I want to learn something ....
16. I like privacy and quiet for working and thinking ....
17. I can pick out individual instruments in complex musical pieces ....
18. I can visualize remembered and constructed scenes easily ....
19. I have a well developed vocabulary and am expressive with it ....
20. I enjoy and value taking written notes ....
21. I have a good sense of balance and enjoy physical movements ....
22. I can discern pattern and relationships between experiences or things ....
23. In teams, I co-operate and build on the ideas of others ....
24. I am observant and will often see things others miss ....
25. I get restless easily ....
26. I enjoy working or learning independently of others ....
27. I enjoy making music ....
28. I have a facility with numbers and mathematical problems ....

Scoring:

Linguistic Statements: 5, 9, 19 & 20.

Total: ....

Mathematical and Logical Statements: 6, 11, 22 & 28.

Total: ....

Visual and Spatial Statements: 2, 12, 18 & 24.

Total: ....

Musical Statements: 4, 10, 17 & 27.

Total: ....

Interpersonal Statements: 3, 8, 13 & 23.

Total: ....

Intrapersonal Statements: 7, 15, 16 & 26.

Total: ....

Kinesthetic Statements: 1, 14, 21 & 25.

Total: ....

Multiple Intelligence Wheel

By taking the numerical score against each intelligence from the questionnaire,
plotting it on the wheel and shading each segment you will get a visual representation
of your balance of intelligences according to Howard Gardner's theory.

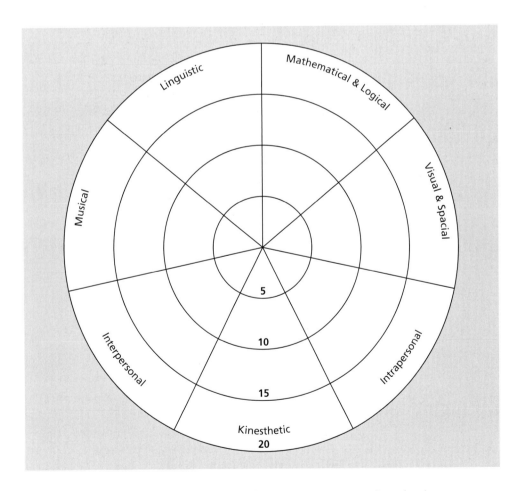

Thanks to Network Educational Press Ltd for permission to reproduce the above
questionnaire from: Smith, Alistair (1998) Accelerated Learning in Practice (pp. 187-189).

The Emotional Competence Framework

Personal Competence (How We Manage Ourselves)

Self-Awareness: (knowing one's internal states, preferences, resources and intuitions).

1. Emotional Awareness (recognizing one's emotions and their effects).
2. Accurate self-assessment (knowing one's strengths and limits).
3. Self-confidence: strong sense of one's self-worth and capabilities.

Self-Regulation: (managing one's internal states, impulses and resources).

1. Self-control: keeping disruptive emotions and impulses in check.
2. Trustworthiness: maintaining standards of integrity and honesty.
3. Conscientiousness: taking responsibility for personal performance.
4. Adaptability: Flexibility in handling change.
5. Innovation: being comfortable with novel ideas, approaches and new information.

Motivation: emotional tendencies that guide or facilitate reaching goals.

1. Achievement drive: striving to improve or meet a standard of excellence.
2. Commitment: aligning with the goals of the group or organization.
3. Initiative: readiness to act on opportunities.
4. Optimism: persistence in pursuing goals despite obstacles and setbacks.

Social Competence (These Competencies Determine How We Handle Relationships)

Empathy: Awareness of others' feelings and perspectives
and taking an active interest in their concerns.

1. Understanding others: sensing others' feelings and perspectives,
   and taking an active interest in their concerns.
2. Developing others: sensing others' developmental needs and bolstering their abilities.
3. Service orientation: anticipating, recognizing, and meeting customers' needs.
4. Leveraging diversity: cultivating opportunities through different kinds of people.
5. Political awareness: reading a group's emotional currents and power relationships.

Social Skills: Adeptness at inducing desirable responses in others.

1. Influence: wielding effective tactics for persuasion.
2. Communication: listening openly and sending convincing messages.
3. Conflict management: negotiating and resolving disagreements.
4. Leadership: inspiring and guiding individuals and groups.
5. Change catalyst: initiating or managing change.
6. Building bonds: nurturing instrumental relationships.
7. Collaboration and cooperation: working with others toward shared goals.

8. Team capabilities: creating group synergy in pursuing collective goals.

From: Goleman (1998) Working with Emotional Intelligence.

List Of Feeling Words

Accepting
Afraid
Agitated
Ambivalent
Angry
Annoyed
Anxious
Arrogant
At peace

Belittled
Blasé
Bored
Brave

Cautious
Confident
Confused
Congenial
Content
Competent
Co-operative

Defensive
Delighted
Depressed
Disappointed
Disillusioned
Distrusting
Doubtful

Elated
Empathetic
Energetic
Enthusiastic
Excited

Free
Frightened
Fulfilled
Frustrated

Genuine

Happy
Honest
Honoured
Hopeful/less

Hurt

Ignored
Impressed
Indignant
Inferior
Inhibited
Insecure
Intolerant

Jealous
Jubilant
Jumpy

Knowledgeable

Listless
Lonely
Loving

Malevolent
Mischievous
Miserable
Moody
Morose

Nasty
Naughty
Numbed

Optimistic
Overjoyed
Overlooked

Perplexed
Pleased
Picked on
Put on

Relaxed
Rejected
Relieved
Repulsed
Resentful
Respectful

Sad
Satisfied

Shame
Shocked
Sorrow
Spiteful
Superior
Suspicious
Strong
Successful

Tense
Tolerant
Tough
Tranquil
Trusting

Unhappy
Unloved

Valiant
Vain
Valued
Vengeful

Wan
Warmth
Wary
Whimsical
Worried
Worthless
Yearning

Appendix 12

List Of Interventions To Facilitate Learning

Advising

Brainstorm

Challenge/confront
Circular questioning
Coaching

Demonstrating
Drama therapy
Draw (art)
Dreamwork

Empty chair work
Experiment (try differently)

Facilitate internal reflection
Feedback
Film
Fly on wall client
Force-field analysis

Give reading

Images (imaging)
Immediacy
Information giving
Instructing
Interpersonal Process Recall
Intuition

Lecturing

Metaphor
Modelling

Narrative (Story-Telling)

Paradox
Paradoxical injunctions
Parallel process
Play
Poetry
Process issues

Reflection
Role-play
Role-reversal

Sculpt (animals)
Sharing own experience
Silence (be still)
Skills training
Socratic questioning
Song (music)
Stakeholder perspectives
Summarising
Suspend
SWOT

Exercise

Add other methods that would facilitate learning.

Theory Of Core Qualities

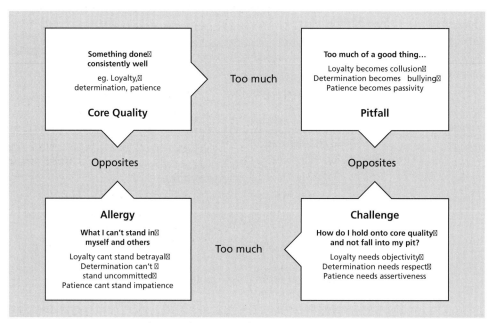

Theory of Core Qualities (Ofman, 2001)

My Core Quality	My Pitfall	My Challenge	My Allergy

How can I meet the challenge of holding my core quality without falling into being too much of a good or bad thing?

Drivers Checklist

Put a tick against any item that generally applies to you. Colleagues who know you well can also be invited to assist you in this process.

Please others:

1. I smile or laugh a lot when I am talking to someone ☐
2. I leave when things begin to go wrong to avoid conflict ☐
3. I nod my head a lot when I talk or frequently say "You know" ☐
4. I dress carefully to show that I have my own special style ☐
5. I laugh to smooth things over when I am a little nervous ☐
6. I say complimentary things before asking for something I want ☐
7. I act 'cheerful' to cover over my bad feelings in meetings ☐
8. I automatically give first priority to others whatever the situation ☐
9. I am usually restless when I am by myself ☐
10. I often volunteer to do things that others are reluctant to do ☐

Be Perfect:

1. I am very aware of the mistakes of others and often point these out ☐
2. I am often early for meetings and get impatient with latecomers ☐
3. I tidy up regularly and hesitate to use a clean waste basket ☐
4. I believe that attention to detail is vital to success at work ☐
5. I set very high standards for myself and others ☐
6. I collect interesting information and display this to others ☐
7. I get things exactly right and do not make mistakes ☐
8. I do not trust others to do things well enough ☐
9. I have difficulty in delegating tasks to others ☐
10. My motto is: "If a thing is worth doing it's worth doing well" ☐

Be Strong:

1. I am outwardly calm even when upset ☐
2. I consider carefully and take my time before making a decision ☐
3. I often do without things that I could easily afford or access ☐
4. I regularly carry around more in my briefcase than I need ☐
5. I make the best of a bad situation for far too long ☐
6. I do things for others that they should do for themselves ☐
7. I am extra cautious in most situations ☐
8. I can hide my feelings by my facial expression ☐
9. I can be physically uncomfortable for a long time without noticing too much ☐
10. I believe in not complaining in the face of adversity ☐

Hurry up:

1. I hurry even when it does not matter ☐
2. I do not get around to buying clothes that I need for work ☐
3. I am the first to say: "Are you ready? Let's go" ☐
4. I am quick to be on the go whatever the occasion ☐

5. I frequently tap my fingers, wiggle my feet or jiggle my knees up and down ☐
6. I do too much too fast and get exhausted ☐
7. I bump into things or people when I am in a hurry ☐
8. I interrupt people to hurry them along or start leaving before they finish ☐
9. I pace back and forth while I am waiting ☐
10. I walk fast, work fast, eat fast, and talk fast ☐

Try Hard:

1. I have trouble finishing things ☐
2. I often realize that I have done something the hard way ☐
3. I tell myself "This time I will do it right" and then I don't ☐
4. I have difficulty accepting when things go smoothly for others ☐
5. I delay getting around to important things for too long and sabotage myself ☐
6. I ease off the effort and delay when I get close to finishing something ☐
7. I am often disorganized and have papers strewn all over my desk ☐
8. I let jobs accumulate and then avoid them ☐
9. I am sometimes quite late for meetings or do not get there at all ☐
10. I delay too long before starting on a job ☐

Score one point for each item that you have ticked. Scores over five will give you an indication of your 'favourite' drivers. These are the drivers that are most important to you; you can then evaluate with your coach to what extent they help or hinder your performance.

(Modelled after 'Drivers Checklist' 1986 by Joseph William Hazell: TAJ. Vol 19: 4).

Preparing For Your First Executive Coaching Session

Session 1: Date and Time with (Name of Executive
Coach) plus address and telephone number

Introduction

A Coaching Contract with three parties has been agreed on (date). The
Organizational/Commissioning Client (Name) who is paying the fees, the
Coachee (Name) and the Coach (Name of Executive Coach)

We have contracted for XXX sessions authorized by the organizational
client should we want them. Each session will last 2 hours and normally
take place at the address above. We will discuss confidentiality and any
reporting processes. There will be a review at the end of the 4th session.

What is executive coaching? Here is my definition…

The coaching process, when commissioned by an organizational client, is a means
of developing an individual within the organization in order that they perform more
effectively and reach goals. Goals may be those the organization would like the coachee
to reach and/or goals that the coachee wants personally to reach in a work related
context. It is normal to have some connected between work and life. Coaching is
performance oriented, seeks positive change and action and is generally short term.

How does it work?

Coaching is an explicit contractual relationship which works best when the coachee
chooses to be coached, is involved in choosing their coach and chooses to learn.

It also works best when the coach learns how to join the coachee
in their world and in the coachee's learning style.

What happens?

As your coach I will provide a quiet place where we can work with minimum risk
of interruption. I will provide a 'contract' which outlines how we might work
together. We can discuss and finalize this on the day. For now and in brief - I will
seek to facilitate your learning using a range of interventions including questions
and supportive challenging. I will listen carefully to your stories and what you want
to achieve, help you formulate goals and actions that you are willing to commit
to taking. I will give you constructive feedback and I will ask for feedback.

Preparation.

It benefits the process hugely if the coachee prepares for each session, keeps
notes and puts into practice between sessions the actions s/he decides on.

For your first session there are four things to do:

1. Find out if there are any specific goals the commissioning client (your boss maybe) would like you to reach.
2. Find out what level of 'progress reporting' your boss is expecting (if any) but avoid lengthy discussion.
3. Decide for yourself what goals you would like to reach and in particular what you want from the first session. Eg. clarity about your priorities
4. Think about how you learn - what helps you learn, what blocks your learning.

Exercise to help prepare.

I enclose an exercise in preparing for coaching reproduced from Michael Carroll's new book (Becoming an Executive Coachee, 2008) with his permission. This may well help.

(Our thanks to John Nixon for permission to reproduce the above)

Appendix 16

My Learning Log

What happened?

What did I learn?

How and when will I use what I have learned?

How can I develop myself in this area?

Questions To Help You Prepare For Your Coaching Session

Contracting: Starting with the end in mind and agreeing
about how you will get there together.

1. How do you want to use your time?
2. What do you most need to achieve in this session?
3. How could your executive coach (or someone else) be most valuable to you?
4. What in particular do you want to focus on during your coaching session?
5. What would make this session a success, both for you and for your organization?
6. What do you want to have achieved or shifted before leaving here?

Generating insights into the situation

1. Are there other people involved that you have not mentioned?
2. How do other people (your boss, your colleagues, your team) see the satiation?
3. Can you summarize this issue?

Exploring 1: Understanding the personal impact the situation is having on you

1. How are you feeling right now?
2. Are there any feelings you have not expressed?
3. Does this person remind you of anyone?
4. What is it you would like to say to this person?
5. What in you is standing in the way of resolving this?

Exploring 2: Challenging to create new possibilities
for future action in resolving the situation

1. Who might be of help to you that you have not consulted?
2. Who has the information you need?
3. Who has the skills you need?
4. Who has the power to affect change in this situation?
5. Can you think of four different ways of tackling this situation?
6. What is the wildest option you can think of for dealing with this situation?
7. How would someone you admire deal with this situation?

Supporting you in committing to a way ahead and creating the next step

1. What are the pros and cons of each possible strategy?
2. What is your long-term objective?
3. What is the first step you need to take?
4. When precisely are you going to do that?
5. Who needs to be involved, consulted or informed?
6. Is your plan realistic? What is the percentage chance of your succeeding?
7. What do you need to do right now to radically increase
   the percentage chance of success?

Rehearse your opening line right now, as if I am the person you need to talk to.

Review: Taking Stock

1. What have you decided to do next?
2. What have you learned from this session?
3. In what way have you increased your ability to handle similar situations?
4. What did you find helpful about this coaching process?
5. What did you find difficult about this coaching process?
6. What would you like to improve or do differently the next time you have coaching with your executive coach?
7. When are where are you going to review this experimental plan you have just committed to?
8. Are you going to have another executive coaching session, if so when and where?

(Adapted from: Hawkins and Smith, 2006:pp.33-35)

Appendix 18

Statement On Best Ethical Practice

The UK branch of the International Coach Federation; the Association for Professional Executive Coaching and Supervision; the European Mentoring and Coaching Council UK and the Association for Coaching (AC) have signed a statement "synthesising the best ethical practice of all the professional bodies" at a meeting on 28 January 2008

Statement Of Shared Professional Values

Purpose

This statement has been agreed by the coaching professional bodies in the UK who cooperate to enhance the reputation of the coaching industry.

In the emerging profession of coaching, we believe that:

1. Every coach, whether charging fees for coaching provided to individuals or organizations or both, is best served by being a member of a professional body suiting his/her needs
2. Every coach needs to abide by a code of governing ethics and apply acknowledged standards to the performance of their coaching work
3. Every coach needs to invest in their ongoing continuing professional development to ensure the quality of their service and their level of skill is enhanced
4. Every coach has a duty of care to ensure the good reputation of our emerging profession

The following are fundamental principles by which we expect our members to operate:

Meta Principle: To continually enhance the competence and reputation of the coaching profession

Principle One: Reputation

Every coach will act positively and in a manner that increases the public's understanding and acceptance of coaching

Principle Two: Continuous Competence Enhancement

Every coach accepts the need to enhance their experience, knowledge, capability and competence on a continuous basis

Principle Three: Client Centred

Every client is creative, resourceful and whole and the coach's role is to keep the development of that client central to his/her work, ensuring all services provided are appropriate to the client's needs

Principle Four: Confidentiality And Standards

Every coach has a professional responsibility (beyond the terms of the contract with the client) to apply high standards in their service provision and behaviour. He/she needs to be open and frank about methods and techniques used in the coaching process, maintain only appropriate records and to respect the confidentiality a) of the work with their clients and b) or their representative body's members information

Principle Five: Law And Diversity

Every coach will act within the Laws of the jurisdictions within which they practice and will also acknowledge and promote diversity at all times

Principle Six: Boundary Management

Every coach will recognize their own limitations of competence and the need to exercise boundary management. The client's right to terminate the coaching process will be respected at all times, as will the need to acknowledge different approaches to coaching which may be more effective for the client than their own. Every endeavour will be taken to ensure the avoidance of conflicts of interest

Principle Seven: Personal Pledge

Every coach will undertake to abide by the above principles that will complement the principles, codes of ethics and conduct set out by their own representative body to which they adhere and by the breach of which they would be required to undergo due process

Published: 25 February 2008

Epilogue

We hope you have found this manual helpful as you engage as an executive coachee in the coaching process. Our aim has been to support you in becoming a "learning partner" in executive coaching the purpose of which is to enable you to learn better, learn more and learn at even greater depth. Ultimately, that will contribute to your personal and professional development and the goals of your company or organization.

Throughout we have placed the central focus point of coaching on the theme of learning. We end where we started, that executive coaching is a form of personalized learning tailor-made for you. Your task as coachee is to ensure you have the relationship, the environment and the support of your organization to make the best use of coaching. We know that's a burden at times and it should not always fall to you to have to put the above in place. However, it is a learning "partnership" and at times responsibility means that you need to change your executive coach to get what you want – certainly, you may need to re-negotiate the roles, tasks and arrangements involved. We want you to be a demanding executive coachee. Executive coaching is too important an investment to be either another fad or a waste of your time. The executive coaching is for you and for your organization – make sure its worthwhile and a very good return on investment. We know it can be.

Michael Carroll & Maria Gilbert

September 2008

About the Authors

Michael Carroll PhD

Michael is a Fellow of the British Association for Counselling, a Chartered Counselling Psychologist and a BACP Senior Registered Practitioner. He is an Accredited Executive Coach and an Accredited Executive Coach Supervisor with APECS (Association for Professional Executive Coaches and Supervisors). Michael is Visiting Industrial Professor in the Graduate School of Education, University of Bristol and the winner of the 2001 British Psychological Society Award for Distinguished Contributions to Professional Psychology

Maria Gilbert MA

Maria is a Chartered Clinical Psychologist, a UKCP registered integrative psychotherapist and a BACP accredited supervisor. Maria is Joint Head of the Integrative Department and the Supervision Training at Metanoia Institute in West London. She also co-heads the M.Sc. /MA in Coaching Psychology at Metanoia Institute, and is a Visiting Professor at Middlesex University